Con[t

Your active body

This book tells you how your body moves. It starts with an explanation of the individual parts such as the skeleton, muscles, tendons and ligaments, and then goes on to explain how they work together in a smooth coordinated fashion, allowing you to lift a cup of tea to your lips without pouring it into your lap.

Section Two deals with how you can improve the function of your body, for example, in training for sport. Section Three looks at common disorders which affect your body such as backache with advice on how to avoid these common problems or how to alleviate them if you are already a sufferer. Section Four looks at the problems that are attributable more to bad luck than anything else.

Structure of your moving body

The framework of your body is made up of a bony skeleton consisting of over 200 bones which are usually in pairs. They connect one with the other at joints. There are many different forms of joints, some allowing a great deal of movement, and some almost none at all (see pages 12-13).

The bones are held together at these joints by strong bands of fibrous tissue called ligaments, the size, proportion and strength of which very much dictate the stability and movement of the joint.

Movement is achieved by the muscles under voluntary (conscious) control. These attach to the bones either side of a joint so that contraction of the muscle pulls the two bones closer together causing movement. The muscles may attach directly onto the bone or via a long thin fibrous structure called a tendon.

The advantage of a muscle pulling through a tendon in that the tendon takes up less space so that, for example, in the wrist and fingers where space is limited, many individual muscle functions can act via long thin tendons (see page 16). Another advantage is that they are able to pull round corners creating a pulley effect in certain situations such as in the orbit (socket of the eye) and at the shoulder. Ligaments, therefore, attach bone to bone, tendons attach muscle to bone.

The bones, joints, muscles, ligaments and tendons,

with their controlling nerve supply, make up the components of the mechanism of body movement or in medical terms, the musculo-skeletal system. These structures will now be dealt with in greater detail.

Bones

The popular image of the human skeleton is a very familiar one with its skull, spine, vertebral bodies, ribs and limbs. However, the fact that it can survive for hundreds, and in some cases thousands, of years after death, implies that in life it is a dead, stiff and dry structure. Nothing could be further from the truth.

Bone is alive and supplied with nerves and blood vessels. It is wet and slightly bendable. The body is constantly breaking it down and rebuilding it throughout life and although this may seem less apparent in the bone than it does in the skin, the analogy of comparing the skeleton to a motorway is very apt. It is constantly being dug up and rebuilt in patches so that over the course of a decade or so it is effectively a whole new structure.

This concept is very important in understanding problems such as osteoporosis (see page 66) because it explains how proper body management and appropriate exercise can maintain the strength of bones just as it does with muscles. Exercise maintains the use of the skeleton so that the build-up versus breakdown ratio is kept in a healthy balance.

Bone has several important functions. Firstly, it supports the human frame and allows the complex movement that is enjoyed by the human body. Secondly, it provides space in the marrow cavities for the production of blood, the red marrow being the only source of blood production in the adult. Thirdly, it provides the body with a reservoir of calcium which is needed for various important chemical reactions in the body outside the bone. Finally, it forms a protection for the central nervous system in the form of the brain and spinal cord which are housed within the skull and vertebral column as well as providing protection and support for the special senses, the eyes, ears and organs of balance etc.

Bone worker cells (osteoblasts and osteoclasts)
Although the bone cells remain alive within the bone, most of the actual building and breaking up of bone is done by two linked cells, 'bone eaters' (osteoclasts) and 'bone builders' (osteoblasts). These function in small teams working their way through the bone, constantly breaking it down and rebuilding it, much like the crew of men preparing a road and in this way the bone remodels itself many times throughout one's life.

Bone structure

The actual substance of bone is made up of two main components, bone protein and collagen. There are a number of bone proteins and their individual structure is not relevant here but these are the materials which are calcified (full of calcium) and therefore hard. The collagen forms long, thin fibres which are extremely strong. The two are enmeshed together and act like reinforced concrete. The bone protein (matrix) is like the concrete itself and the collagen fibres like the steel reinforcing wires. This structure confers on the bone considerable strength with slight bending properties.

Within this bone material are scattered bone cells (osteocytes). These are very sparse compared with cells in other organs such as the liver or kidney, but nevertheless, although they appear widely spaced in their own little holes in the bone (lacunae), they are interconnected by thin projections (processes) as if they were 'holding hands' throughout the bone and keeping in touch. Although the bone may appear to be inert these cells remain alive within it.

Articular cartilage

Articular cartilage is another specialized material in your active body and is the slippery, shiny surface that covers the bones at the synovial joints (which you can see on the joint of a leg of lamb). The word cartilage is used in its proper sense and should not be confused with the cartilages in the knee (medical name menisci) which are discussed on page 25.

Articular cartilage is a very shiny white material which covers the bone end and is about one millimeter thick in small joints and several millimeters thick in larger ones. Articular cartilage moving on articular cartilage is six times more slippery than ice sliding on ice. This allows the joint almost frictionless movement.

The articular cartilage achieves this because of its unique construction. It is made up of two principal proteins, collagen and proteoglycans. The high tensile strength collagen forms a mesh in the cartilage entrapping the large sponge-like proteins which attract water. The water is soaked up and the cartilage swells until it reaches a point where the collagen net prevents further expansion. So tightly packed with water is the articular cartilage, that it feels quite hard to the touch.

Unfortunately, unlike bone, articular cartilage has a very limited ability to repair itself if damaged. If bone is lost in an injury it will regrow to be a perfectly normal functional structure in due course, whereas in articular cartilage, although there will be some repair attempted by the body, the wonderful shiny surface will never be completely restored. The joint will be permanently damaged and may go on to give rise to arthritis. This is the reason why injury to a joint can be so disastrous.

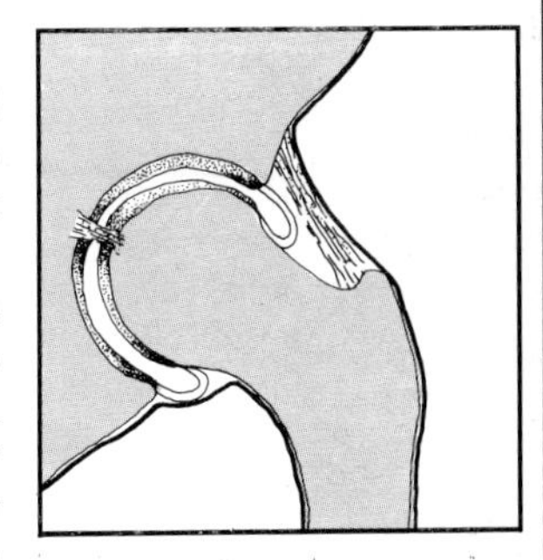

Synovial fluid
The articular cartilage is constantly bathed in a highly slippery fluid called synovial fluid which is produced by the lining of the joint. This fluid is yellowish in appearance and feels like oil, which in many respects is exactly what it is. It also has another important function above that of its lubricating properties. Because the articular cartilage structure prevents blood vessels getting to the surface, the nourishment comes via the synovial fluid. Normal joint movement, therefore, is important in keeping the articular surface healthy.

Tendons

The difference between a tendon and a ligament is that a tendon runs from a muscle to a bone, and a ligament spans joints and runs from bone to bone. Nevertheless, the structure of tendons and ligaments is rather similar and consists of many parallel longitudinal bundles of collagen. Once again, this remarkable material is perfectly suited to its task, being very strong under tension but flexible to allow movement. In the case of ligaments, this allows complex joints, such as the knee, to be firmly held in place and stable from side to side, but allows a great range of movements backwards and forwards.

In the case of tendons, these long, thin structures can take the full pull of a muscle, often round a pulley of bone, to exert the muscle's force at a different angle. This is especially so in the fingers where all the main powerful finger movement muscles are in the forearm and long, thin tendons stretch into the fingertips through multiple pulleys to allow precise yet powerful movement.

Tendons differ from ligaments in one very important way. Because of the pulley-type arrangement of many tendons, they are surrounded by a synovial sheath, a lubricating tube through which the tendons run. The fluid that it produces is very similar to that produced by the lining of the joint. If the tendon is overused, this lining can

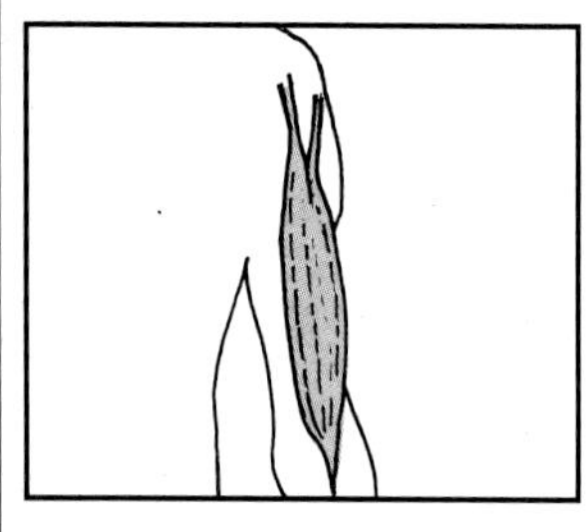

Voluntary muscle
As the name suggests, this responds to your conscious commands, although one does not have to actively think about moving individual muscles when walking or running. It is also possible to exert voluntary control over the muscles of respiration so that you can hold your breath, but fortunately between these moments you breathe without having to think about it.

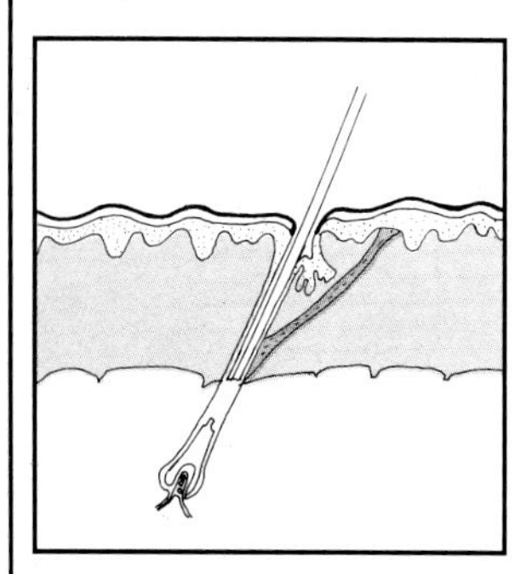

Involuntary muscle
This is the muscle that is not under your conscious command and is widespread throughout the body in such areas as your gut, in the blood vessels and attached to the hairs of your skin.

become inflamed and a condition known as tenosynovitis can ensue.

Muscles

The previous section detailed the fine structure of those materials in the body which allow movement to occur. Muscles are the specialized tissues which actually cause the movement. There are three basic forms of muscle within the body.

- Voluntary or striated muscle
- Involuntary or smooth muscle
- Heart or cardiac muscle

Voluntary muscle

The striated muscle is what a lay person thinks of when the word 'muscle' is used, for example, your biceps and triceps are made up of striated muscle. It is called striated because under the microscope it looks striped. This is due to the arrangement of the specialized proteins, actin and myosin, which are arranged in interlocking patterns and have the extraordinary property that when stimulated by a nerve signal they can draw together thus shortening the muscle and activating movement.

Not surprisingly, this is an enormously energy-consuming process. The muscle cells are therefore thick with tiny power packs called mitochondria, sub-cellular particles whose sole function is to produce energy from glucose and oxygen. When the muscle receives the electrical signal the energy is released from the power pack, the actin and myosin close ranks, the muscle shortens and movement occurs. This clearly takes much less time in real life than it does to read a single letter of this description.

In order to provide the muscle with the huge amount of energy, glucose and oxygen it requires for movement, the blood supply is very extensive. In fact, muscles need more blood size for size than any other part of the body. The muscles are also endowed with a rich supply of nerves. This not only allows the muscle to respond to your commands via nerve impulses but also provides sensory feedback to your brain telling you how contracted your muscle is and adding to what is known as proprioception (joint position sense) which tells you where your foot or finger is even when your eyes are closed.

Smooth muscle (involuntary muscle)

This muscle does not appear striped under the microscope and is thus called unstriated or smooth. The muscle responds to various forms of reflex activity and sensory input which you cannot control. Your gut will move your meal down through your intestines whether you think about it or not. Similarly, in very cold weather you will get goose pimples as your body responds to the cool temperature by erecting the hairs over your body to try and trap air against your skin. Apart from getting out of the cold, there is no way you can actively control these small muscles.

Cardiac muscle

Cardiac muscle is in a category all of its own because although it is involuntary, it is also striped in appearance under the microscope like voluntary muscle.

Your heart beats regularly without you having to think about it (those people who can consciously control the rate of their hearts do so by other mechanisms). The heart beats at approximately 70 beats a minute for 70 years and has an extraordinary capacity to do this without tiring. It is generously supplied with blood not from the main chambers of the heart but through vessels running over its surface known as the coronary vessels. It is a clot (thrombosis) in these coronary vessels that gives rise to the typical heart attack.

This has dealt with the basic structure of muscular tissue but much more will be said later about the function of it and how to help to keep it healthy.

Summary

The musculo-skeletal system makes up the bulk of your body and is comprised of specialized material as outlined above, each with a fine composition and structure suited perfectly to the function we require of it. These individual materials are built up into functional units such as whole bones, joints, and subsequently anatomical areas of the spine and limbs.

Anatomy of a bone

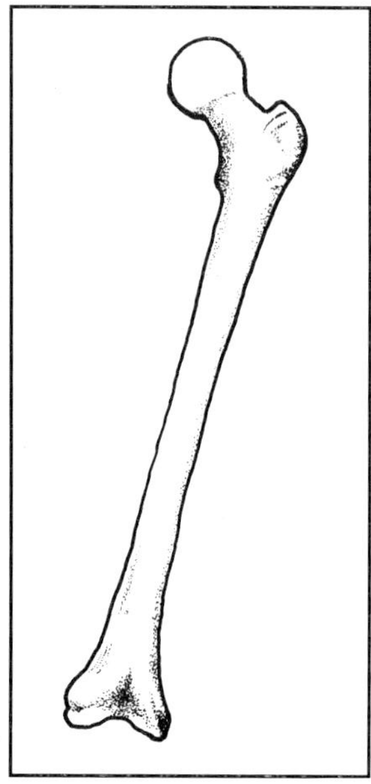

The bone responds to the use that is made of it by building up more strength where it is needed. This gives rise to the characteristic shape of individual bones, thick areas where there is a lot of compression and prominent bulges where a tendon or muscle is inserting and pulling on the bone.

Having seen how the individual cells and matrix go to form the material of bone, we can now look at how this bone material is made up into the structure that we recognize as an individual bone such as the femur in the thigh.

The most obvious and striking feature is that most bones are hollow. The reason for this is principally two-fold. It provides a very strong but light structure like a bamboo pole or scaffolding pole. Hollow tubes are stronger than solid cylinders made from the same material weight for weight.

The space within the bone, the marrow cavity, is for the most part filled with yellow fatty material, but in the central part of the body, especially in the breastbone, spine, pelvis and upper part of the femur, the marrow is red and is the site of blood cell formation. This is a very complex process and is outside the scope of this particular book as it has little bearing on the mechanical features of the skeleton, but it is another example of how ingenious nature is in making use of all available space.

Not only are bones hollow to increase their strength to weight ratio but, depending on their position in the body, their shape is determined by the forces that are put through them. Indeed, it is an important rule in the growing skeleton that the bone will shape itself to those forces that occur throughout childhood. For example, the bones in a functionless limb of a child with polio will be shorter, smaller and thinner than those in a healthy leg.

Structure

As well as the contours and shape dictated by the forces through the bone, the sites of the joints (usually at each end) are also clear. Here the bone is very smooth and beautifully shaped to fit hand in glove with the opposite bone with which it is articulating. The bone is strengthened underneath the articular surface to spread the load across the joint. As well as this shape there are often lumps and projections on the bone known as tubercles and tuberosities to which ligaments, muscles and tendons around the joint attach and these also give rise to familiar patterns on each bone.

Joints

There are over 200 bones in the body ranging enormously in size and shape from a few millimetres to half a metre in length. In general terms they are paired as well as symmetrical. All these bones are joined together to form the skeleton and the form of these joints varies enormously depending on the functional requirement and the way the bones have developed.

Synovial joints

This is the commonest form of joint and has the greatest range of movement between the bones. The bone ends where they join are covered in highly slippery articular cartilage and the surfaces of the bones are carefully matched to provide a snug fit, a good example of which is the ball and socket arrangement of the hip joint. The bone ends, with their articular cartilage covering, are enclosed within a fibrous structure called the joint capsule. The capsule is firmly attached to the bones on either side of the joint and is loose enough to allow movement but strong enough to provide some stability. The capsule may be thickened in various areas to provide extra strength. On the inside of the capsule there is a lining of synovial membrane from which the joint gets its name. This produces the oily fluid which lubricates and nourishes the articular surface.

Ligaments attached either side of the joint provide extra stability where needed and sometimes are merged with the joint capsule itself so the two are almost indistinguishable.

Synovial joint movement

The movement that occurs at the joint depends on a number of factors. First the position of the opposing articular surfaces; second the position of any supporting ligaments; and thirdly the arrangement of the muscles which move the joint itself. These elements all act together to provide the best range of useful movement in the most stable situation. Some of the commonest synovial joints appear on the following pages.

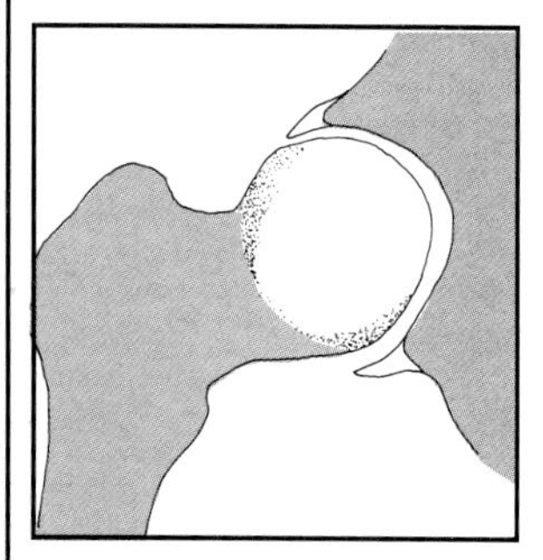

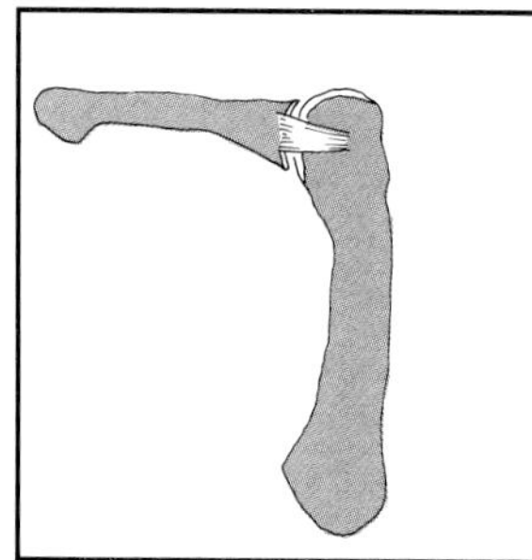

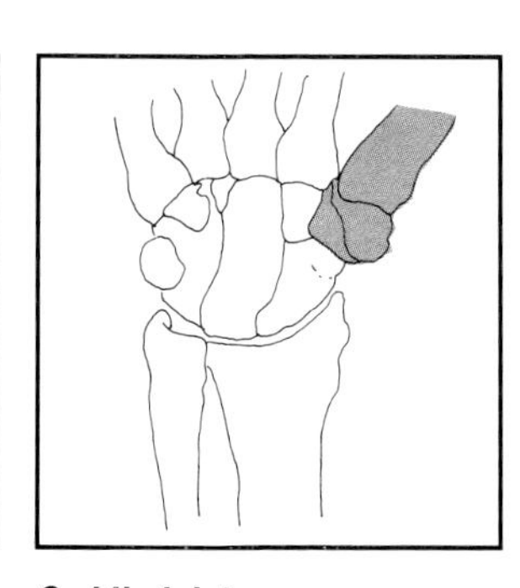

Ball and socket

This is the arrangement of the hip and shoulder joint. The name is self explanatory. The value of such a joint is the enormous range of movement that can be achieved, not only bending and straightening the limb but moving it sideways (abduction and adduction) and also twisting it round (internal and external rotation). This provides enormous freedom of movement and function. The disadvantage, however, is that this type of joint is not as stable and certainly in the case of the shoulder joint dislocation is a very common consequence of injury to the arm.

Hinged joints

Although these are described as hinged joints they have little to do with the hinge we are familiar with in the household. These joints allow basically just one direction of movement. A good example of this are the joints in the fingers. They can bend and straighten but can't move sideways and can't twist. They are fairly stable joints for their size as a result. This side to side stability comes from the strong ligaments on either side of the joints known as collateral ligaments. This term is common to many joints of a similar nature, for example the knee. (The knee joint is not truly a single plane hinge and is a site of common problems.)

Saddle joints

This is a rather unusual arrangement and is the one at the base of the thumb. It's a half-way house between a hinge and a ball and socket joint. It's called a saddle joint because the movement is that of a person sitting on a saddle. They can tip forwards and backwards and slide from side to side but can't rotate. It allows more movement than a simple hinge and is important in the function of the thumb in pinching and gripping.

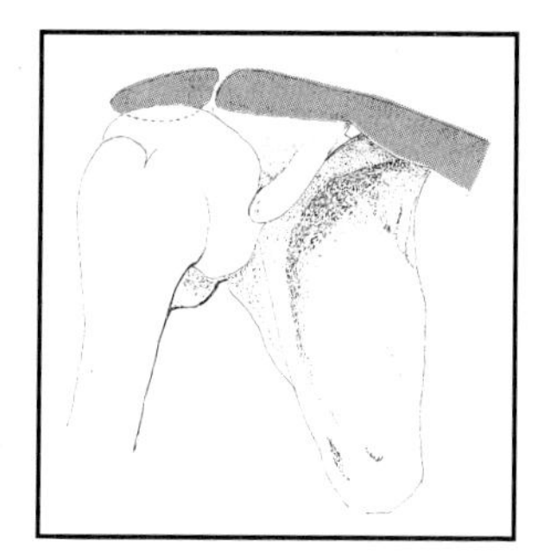

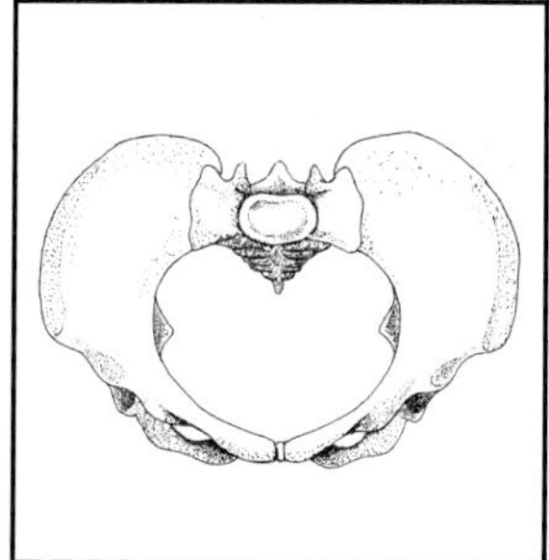

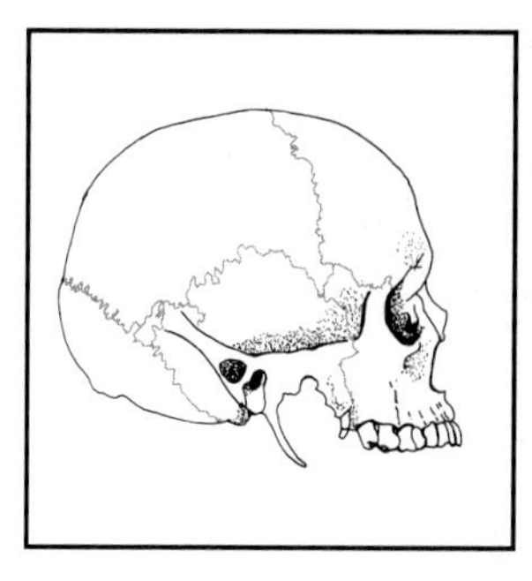

Sliding joints

At the opposite end of the spectrum to the highly mobile synovial ball and socket joint is a simple sliding joint where only a small amount of movement occurs. The bone surfaces once again are covered with articular surface and surrounded by a synovial capsule but the only movement of the two flat surfaces together is a little slipping, sliding or rotating. An example of this is where the collar bone meets the shoulder blade at the point of the shoulder (the acromioclavicular). It allows only a tiny jog of movement between the bones giving some flexibility in the shoulder girdle although the shoulder joint itself provides the mobility for the arm. These joints tend to be well supported by strong ligaments.

Fibrocartilaginous joints (syndesmoses)

Where even less movement is required than can be provided by the slidey, slippery synovial joints a fibrocartilaginous joint is used. These tend to be in the midline of the body, for example, between the bones of the pelvis at the front (the pubic symphysis) and between the back bones. The intervertebral discs are specialized types of this joint. The bone ends are not covered with the shiny articular surface but there is fibrous tissue and some gristly material (fibrocartilage) between the two. Strong ligaments support them. This is a very stable arrangement but also allows a little jog of movement and some shock absorbency and helps transmit the jarring forces of normal walking and running gradually throughout the skeleton.

Simple fibrous joints

These are worth mentioning although they have little to do with movement or function of the musculo-skeletal system. Occasionally bones are joined together by strong, tightly interlocking joints. The most typical example of this is the plates of the skull bones which are joined together in a jigsaw fashion, producing the typical wiggly feature on a skull surface. These are not so much functional arrangements for movement but rather a feature of the way the bones have developed throughout embryological life. No useful movement occurs at these joints. They are completely stable and in the case of the skull are almost impossible to separate even in the dry skeleton.

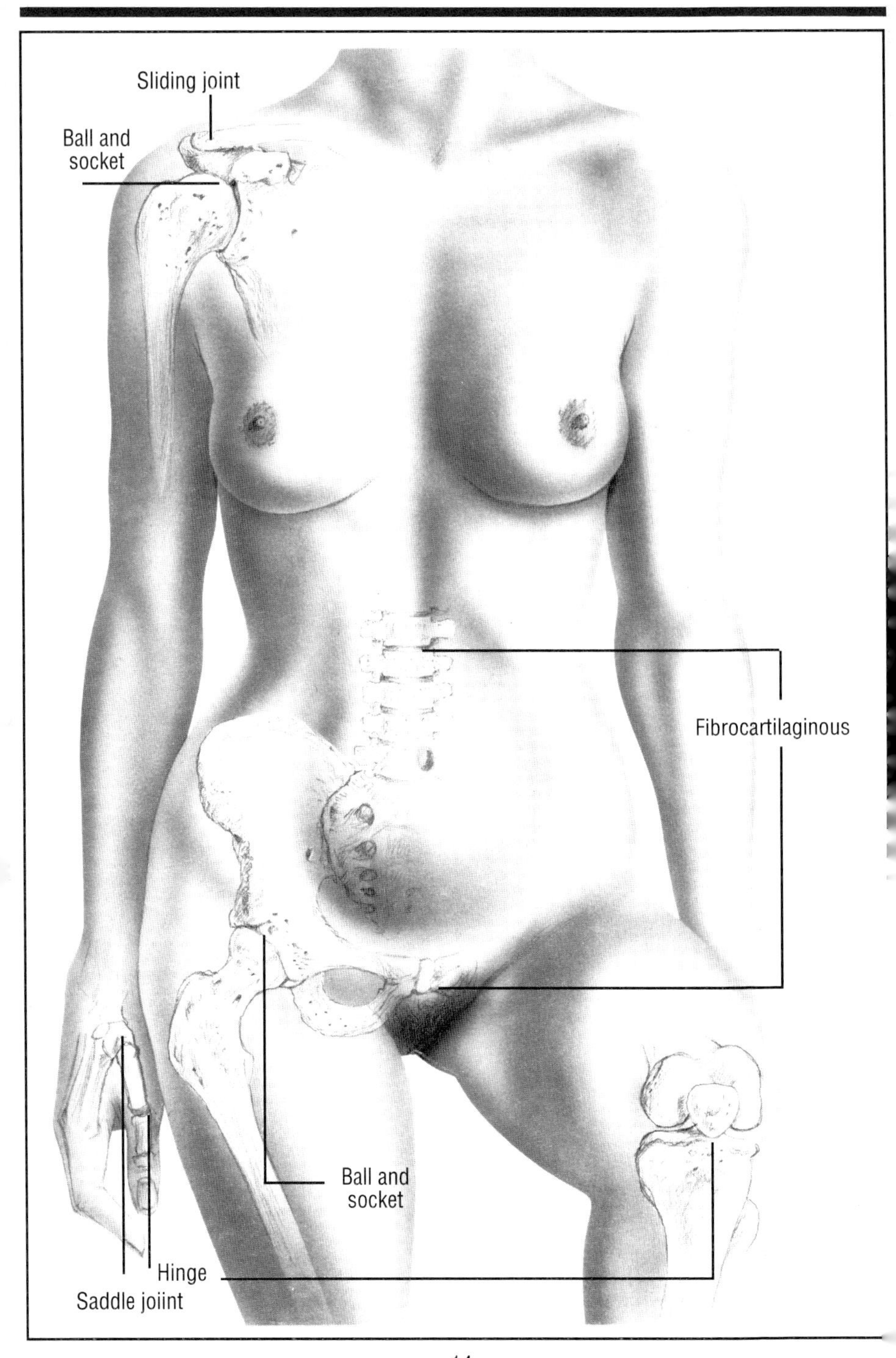
Sliding joint
Ball and socket
Fibrocartilaginous
Ball and socket
Hinge
Saddle joiint

Movement

The basic functioning unit that produces movement consists of a nerve running out from the spinal cord to attach to a number of muscle fibres in the limb or trunk of the body.

The nerve and muscle fibres form what is known as the motor unit. Electrical impulses passing down the nerve fire off the muscle to contract. The number of muscle fibres that an individual nerve supplies varies greatly. In the large muscle of the buttock (the gluteus maximus), one nerve will supply a large number of muscle fibres so there is coordinated, mass action of muscle power, for example, when the sprinter bursts into a 20 mile an hour sprint. At the other end of the spectrum in the small muscles of the hand a nerve may supply only a few fibres so that the very delicate and finely coordinated movements of the violin player, for example, can be achieved.

As well as nerves supplying the muscle to stimulate it to contract there are also sensors within the muscle fibre which feed information back to the spinal cord. This keeps the spinal cord and therefore the brain constantly aware of what the muscle is doing. This feedback arrangement is a very common feature of many activities within the body - one nerve generating activity and another testing, as it were, that the activity has occurred.

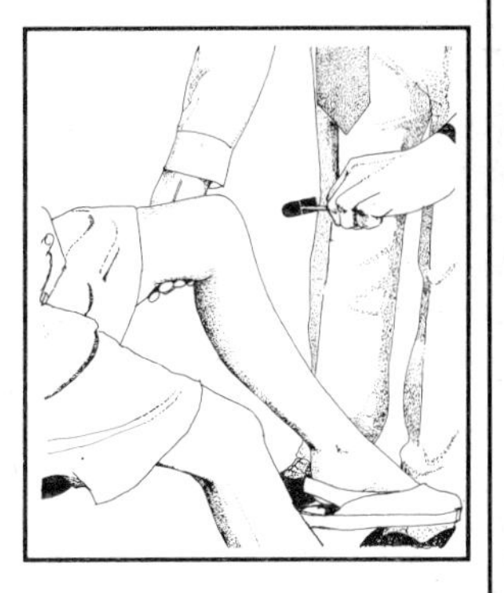

The reflex arc is demonstrated when the doctor tests your 'knee jerk'. Striking your knee tendon with a rubber hammer briefly stretches the muscle in the front of the thigh and automatically (via the reflex arc) makes the muscle contract giving rise to the characteristic jerk. Although you can consciously override this reflex if you choose to, it will occur automatically without your conscious control. Indeed it will still be present even if there has been an injury high up in the spinal cord preventing your active control. By using this reflex the doctor can test the intact nerve and muscle fibres.

The reflex arc

This two-way arrangement also explains how your reflexes work. If a muscle is suddenly stretched, the sense organs within the muscle fire off a nerve sending signals back to the spinal cord. The nerve is connected to the nerve that fires the muscle itself and this causes the muscle to recontract to try and return to its original position. This reflex activity occurs at the level of the spinal cord, i.e. the impulses involved never reach your brain and can occur therefore out of your voluntary control.

Balanced muscle control

Another important principle and reflex which allows for coordinated, smooth movement is that of teams of paired muscles acting together with one another either side of a

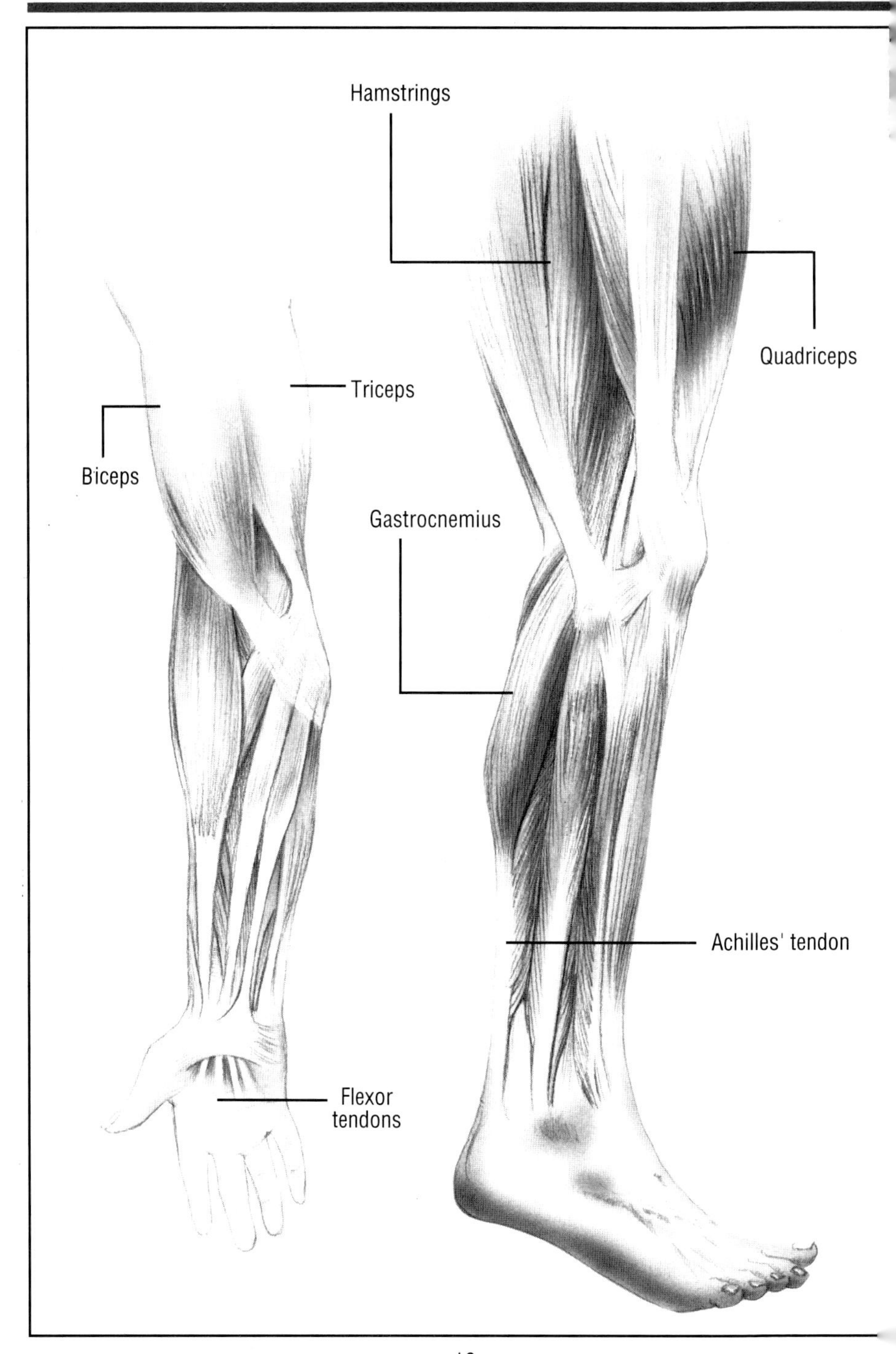
Hamstrings
Quadriceps
Triceps
Biceps
Gastrocnemius
Achilles' tendon
Flexor
tendons

joint. For example, the biceps muscle (at the front of your upper arm) bends the elbow up, the triceps muscle (the muscle behind the arm) straightens it out. Clearly these two muscles would not normally both work together so that there is a system of reflexes which allows one to actively extend or stretch while the other one bends up or flexes. This coordinated pattern of movement once again occurs at a spinal level to some extent although you can override it by conscious decision and tighten up both your biceps and your triceps together if you want to lock your arm rigid.

Joint position sense (proprioception)

As well as sensors in the muscle fibres which respond to muscle stretching, there are also stretch receptors around the joints in the tendons and ligaments. These provide a constant flow of information to the brain about the exact position of the joint and thus your limbs.

This joint position sense is essential for normal function and although it may not be as immediately apparent as the special senses such as sight and hearing, nevertheless the ability to know how near your foot is to the ground without looking at it is clearly very important for normal walking.

Occasionally joint position sense is interfered with, for example, in a sprained ankle when some of the sensory fibres have been damaged. Some people suffer problems of instability of the joint afterwards and complain that their ankles regularly 'go over'. This is not simply due to ligamentous weakness after the sprain, but to the fact that they have lost some of the sensation of knowing where their foot is in relation to their leg. This joint position sense can be trained up by special physiotherapy techniques and will overcome their apparent instability. This illustrates the importance of the muscles in stability and normal function of the joints and also the importance of maintaining these muscles in good shape to prevent injury.

Moving parts

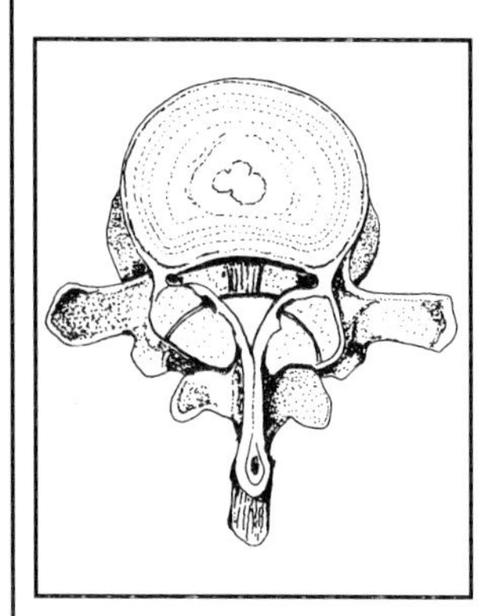

A typical vertebra
The body of the vertebra is the main load bearing area and is roughly cylindrical in shape. Behind it lies a ring of bone. In the spine these rings of bone stack one on top of the other and create a long flexible tube known as the spinal canal. It is within this that the spinal cord runs.

From this ring of bone there are a number of projections, one on either side known as the transverse processes to which the muscles of the spine attach and a single unpaired process which points backwards and slightly downwards, the vertebral spinous process. The ends of this point are easy to feel down the centre of your back. Just like the transverse processes, this is a major attachment for the spinal muscles.

Although individual areas such as the spine, the shoulder or the knee are made up of a number of bones and muscle groups, their individual function is clearly defined, and to understand the problems that can occur in them and how to avoid them, it's valuable to have a working knowledge of the major areas in some detail.

Spine

The spine is a long, strong, bendable structure which runs literally from head to tail (even though the tail is somewhat vestigial in the human). It supports your head at its top end and your pelvis is attached to the lower end. It not only provides mechanical support for the ribs and the other bony structures but also has the very specialized function of being hollow in order to protect and carry the spinal cord which conducts the nerves from the brain to the rest of the body. It is divided up into five segments. The cervical spine (the neck), the thoracic spine in the chest from which the ribs arise, the lumbar spine (the low back), the sacrum (the part of the spine which attaches to the pelvis) and finally the coccyx which is the vestigial tail (in humans this has muscle attachments for the pelvic floor and has nothing to do with spinal movement).

The spine is made up of individual unpaired bones which are stacked one on top of the other. These bones are called vertebrae. Broadly speaking they have similar characteristics throughout the spine but in each area there are particular features of difference.

The intervertebral disc

This is a specialized fibrocartilaginous joint (see page 13). The term disc is rather misleading because although it is disc shaped or slightly kidney shaped, it resembles a bag of thick jelly rather than a solid structure. The bag of thick material itself is called the annulus fibrosus and the jellyish centre the nucleus pulposus. When a disc 'slips', what actually happens is that the bag ruptures and some of the thick jellyish material extrudes and can cause problems by pressing on the spinal nerve.

The cervical spine

Every mammal has seven cervical vertebrae in the neck, even a giraffe. Humans have seven too. The neck is very mobile and allows forwards, backwards and sideways bending, and because of the special arrangement of the vertebrae at the top end, a lot of rotation. Its purpose is to support the head and allow it enormous mobility for the benefit of the special senses such as the eyes which are housed within the skull.

Your head is very heavy and holding it steady and moving it accurately requires the use of many large muscles which make up the bulk of your neck. These attach to the transverse processes and spinous processes of the cervical vertebrae as well as directly on to the skull itself. Joint position sense in the neck is also important and the nerves feeding back to the brain interact with those to the eyes and your sense of balance in the inner ear so that you don't have a sensation of spinning every time you move your head.

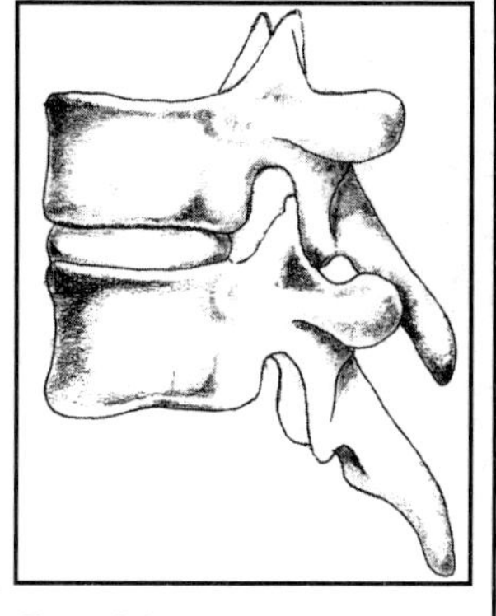

Facet joints

As well as the transverse processes, the ring of bone behind the body supports a pair of synovial joints. These are facet joints and connect one backbone to the other to allow for movement. The vertebrae are also connected with their neighbours above and below by large discs of gristly tissue known as the intervertebral discs. A certain amount of movement can occur at the discs but one of their main functions is to provide a shock absorbing pad to transmit and diffuse the jarring movement s of walking and running.

Thoracic spine

The thoracic spine runs from the base of the neck to the upper back and consists of 12 thoracic vertebrae. Relatively little movement occurs within this segment of the spine but some rotation is possible. Its peculiar characteristic is that the ribs are attached to the transverse processes on either side by synovial joints. This movement of the ribs on the spine produces a bellows effect. In order to take a deep breath, your ribs can lift up and outwards increasing the volume of your chest. It is very unusual to have musculo-skeletal complaints arising from the thoracic spine such as slipped discs and arthritis.

Lumbar spine

In contrast the lower back is one of the commonest causes of disability in the adult population. The lumbar spine consists of five vertebrae although in about one to two percent of people there is some abnormality leaving them with one less or one more lumbar vertebra. These congenital abnormalities may predispose some individuals to backache but are certainly not the cause of most people's problems.

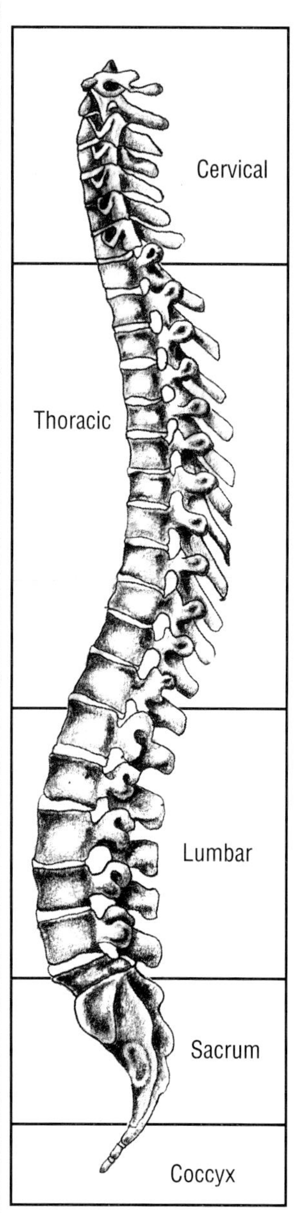

The lumbar vertebrae are the biggest of all and for such a short segment allow a relatively large amount of movement particularly for bending forwards, backwards and side to side.

Sacrum

The sacral part of the spine consists of fused vertebrae so that the sacrum is in fact one large bone. It's attached by its upper edge to the lower lumbar vertebrae, is triangular in shape and attaches on either side to the back of the pelvis, firmly connecting the spine or backbone to the pelvis and thus the lower limbs. These large joints are called the sacro-iliac joints and can be felt as bony ridges at the top of your bottom. They allow very little movement but can be the cause of some problems.

The coccyx

The coccyx is a vestigial tail remnant consisting of four coccygeal vertebrae. They are very small and their residual function in humans is for the attachment of certain muscles in the pelvic floor. At the lowest point of your spine the coccyx occasionally gets bruised by a direct fall onto your bottom and can give rise to persistent and annoying symptoms.

The spinal curves

The spine is naturally curved from front to back. It is curved inwards in the hollow of the lumbar spine and in the cervical spine at the neck. This inwards curve is known as a lordosis. It is curved slightly outwards to form the rounded arc of the back between the shoulder blades (kyphosis). These curves develop slowly from fetal life through childhood to the adult form. Some conditions cause them to be more or less pronounced and their maintenance of good shape is essential for normal spinal posture. Any deviation or curve to the side (scoliosis) is abnormal.

Although the spine is known as the backbone and its backward projecting spinous processes can be felt along the back, the bodies of the vertebrae in the front run almost straight up the centre of your body in the lower lumbar region and in thin people can even be felt through the abdomen. The importance of this is the part the abdominal wall muscles play in maintaining a well-supported and trouble-free spine.

The shoulder and upper arm

The shoulder girdle consists of three bones and their attached muscles, ligaments and joints. The bones are the upper arm bone (humerus), shoulder blade (scapula) and the collar bone (clavicle). These are all connected together around the shoulder joint itself. The important point to note is that apart from a small synovial joint where the collar bone joins to the breastbone (sternum) the shoulder girdle hangs completely free on the top of the ribs supported only by muscles. This allows the whole girdle to be moveable as you can see by shrugging your shoulders up and moving them backwards and forwards. This increases the range of movement for the arm which already has a large range of movement available at the shoulder joint itself.

The opposite however is also true that if these muscles are allowed to become weak the shoulders will droop down and as will be seen later this can give rise to specific problems. The muscles supporting the shoulder girdle run up from the shoulder blade and collar bone into the neck to attach to the cervical spine. These muscles not only support and suspend the shoulder and upper arm but also move it.

The shoulder joint itself is a ball and socket synovial joint allowing a remarkably free range of movement, forwards, backwards, inwards, outwards plus rotation, i.e. twisting. The upper end of the humerus is round and fits into a shallow socket on the outer side of the shoulder blade called the glenoid. In fact this is less of a ball and socket joint and more of a golf ball on a golf tee arrangement because the surface area of the ball is some three times bigger than that of the socket. This makes it relatively unstable although it allows a great deal of movement.

The rotator cuff

To improve the stability there is a group of four muscles which surround the head of the humerus arising from the front and back of the shoulder blade. These muscles encapsulate the head like dynamic guy ropes and during movement take up and pay out in harmony to ensure a stable and free range of movement. These muscles are known as the rotator cuff and despite their elegant design they are unfortunately a site of regular problems. Being very close to the head of the humerus their muscular strength is not enough to give a lot of power to the shoulder movement and this comes from a large muscle over the point of the shoulder called the deltoid which you can easily see and feel. The other strong upper arm muscles, the biceps at the front and the triceps at the back, also have tendons which run across the joint into the shoulder blade and cause movement at the shoulder.

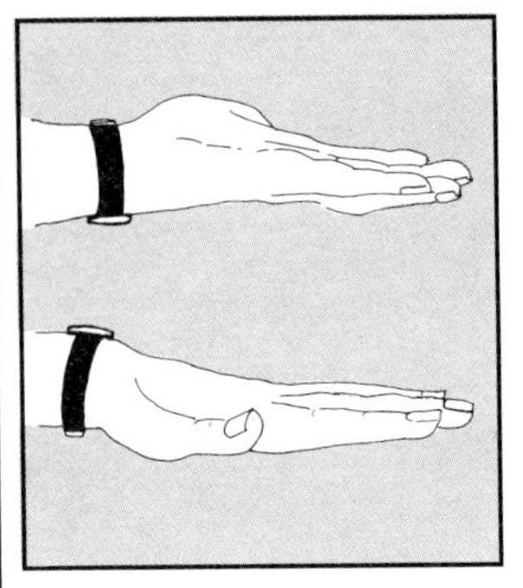

The elbow joint itself not only allows flexion, extension and a hinge pattern but also rotation of the forearm. This is the twisting manoeuvre used in a screwdriving action. This movement is known as pronation and supination and it's critical to the proper use of the forearm and hand. An inability to fully supinate, i.e. to turn the hand outwards, is extremely awkward. You use this movement when receiving change. The two forearm bones can rotate one on the other and this provides the movement. They therefore not only rotate at the elbow but also just above the wrist joint. The wrist joint itself, however, is made up of just the radius and the carpal bones. This joint is another highly mobile synovial joint which allows bending up and back as well as slightly side to side.

Arm and elbow

The biceps and triceps muscles' main function is to flex and extend the elbow. They are powerful muscles which arise not only from the shoulder blade but also from the body of the upper arm bone and attach to the forearm bones. The biceps at the front inserts into the radius and the triceps at the back to the point of the elbow known as the olecranon. The effects of this arrangement is to give a strong lever allowing maximum use of these strong muscles. The triceps and biceps are a matched pair working in harmony.

The hand

The hand is a most remarkable structure as it can provide huge strength with considerable dexterity. It achieves this really in two ways. Firstly its considerable mobility stems from the multiple small bones and joints within the wrist, hand and fingers. Secondly, it is supplied by two basic muscle groups.

The thumb and fingers have long tendons attached to them which run in synovial pulley systems. These tendons run back through the wrist and attach to large muscles in the forearm. The bulk of these muscles is well away from their site of action which leaves the hands small, free and unimpeded yet able to move with tremendous strength. However, there is a second set of muscles, the intrinsic muscles, which actually lie within the palm of the hand itself. These are responsible for the very delicate side to side movements of the fingers which allow fine manipulation. Of course the hand is also a sense organ, the skin over the fingers being the most sensitive in the body.

The pelvis

The pelvis is a massive ring of bone at the lower end of the spine. It not only provides connection for the legs at the hip joints and the necessary muscle and ligament attachments that go with the joint but also provides support for the abdominal and pelvic contents.

The pelvic ring is made up of the two parts of the

pelvis itself which are connected to the spine at the back at the sacrum. At the front of the pelvis these two bones are joined together at a fibrocartilaginous joint known as the pubic symphysis and this can easily be felt in the mid-line at the lower end of your abdomen. A small amount of movement only occurs at this level but, just like the intervertebral discs in the spine, it does provide a shock absorbing capacity. In women the birth canal goes through the pelvic ring and the hormones present during pregnancy slightly slacken the ligaments around the ring making it a little more mobile to ease the birth of the child.

Although little movement occurs between the sacrum and the pelvis, the pelvis does provide a lot of support for muscle attachments of the abdominal muscles and the spinal muscles. These muscles, which are set some way away from the spine, act as very efficient guy ropes in supporting the lower lumbar region.

The hip

The hip joint is the largest joint in the body and is a stable ball and socket joint. It has a remarkable range of movement and its true potential can be seen in ballet dancers. Its principal function, however, is to provide a lever point for walking, running and jumping, and it has to take the whole weight of the body during these manoeuvres.

It is surrounded by large muscles to provide this movement. The buttock muscle (gluteus maximus) is the biggest muscle in the body and it extends or straightens the leg. The muscles of the upper thigh, the quadriceps at the front and the hamstrings at the back, in some part also span the hip joint and help flexion and extension. Lifting the leg out sideways (abduction) is performed by the gluteus medius and minimus muscles and these attach to a large bony protuberance at the top of the femur called the greater trochanter. This can also easily be felt and is the point of the hip on which you lie when you are on your side. Many people call this bone the hip but in fact the true hip joint is much deeper and pain arising from it is usually felt in the groin rather than over the trochanter region.

The thigh and knee

The femur, which runs from the hip to the knee joint, is the longest bone in the body and not surprisingly the muscles overlying it are also the longest. To the front of the thigh are the quadriceps and as their name suggests these are four muscles that act in concert. They attach to the front of the thigh and one of them spans the hip joint at the top. They all attach via the quadriceps tendon to the kneecap and from that to the front of the shin.

They are powerful straighteners of the knee joint. Their function is crucial to a healthy and stable knee. They act in synchrony with the muscles at the back of the thigh, the hamstring muscles. This is also a large group of muscles which tends to act together and the tendons of them all can be felt on either side of the back of the knee where they span the joint and attach to the back of the upper part of the lower leg bones, tibia and fibula. They are powerful benders of the knee and they too are critical to the normal functioning of the knee joint. These large mass actioned muscles are supplied by nerves running down from the spine, the femoral nerve to the quadriceps and the sciatic nerve to the hamstrings. The sciatic nerve is often the site of pain (sciatica) caused by pressure within the spine as we will see later. It is the largest nerve in the body and at the site of the upper part of the thigh is about the size of your little finger in diameter.

Knee joint

The knee is an extremely complex joint and the cause of much trouble to sportsmen and women. The joint is made up of the femur above, the tibia below and the patella or kneecap in front. The ends of the femur are rounded off as paired structures called femoral condyles and these give rise to the familiar bumps to the end of the bone. These are covered in articular cartilage and slide and roll on the almost flat upper surface of the tibia which is also covered in articular cartilage. This movement principally gives rise to bending and straightening in a hinge fashion.

The joint is not a true hinge as a certain amount of rotation also occurs as the knee fully locks out straight.

This rotation is critical to the tightening and the stability of the knee when it is fully straight.

The menisci of the knee

The arrangement of these two round femoral condyles moving on a relatively flat surface presents the joint with some problems and to improve the congruity of the joint and its stability as well as the nutrition of the articular cartilage, it has two washers within it.

These are shaped like the segments of an orange and are situated between the shiny surfaces of the femur and the tibia. These are the knee menisci or 'knee cartilages'. The term 'cartilage' is popular and clearly understood by most lay people and sportsmen and women, but it can be somewhat confusing when we also use the term to describe the material 'articular cartilage' which is completely different and which is the shiny covering of the bone ends at synovial joints. For the purposes of this book the correct term is used to avoid confusion and at relevant points will include in brackets 'knee cartilages'.

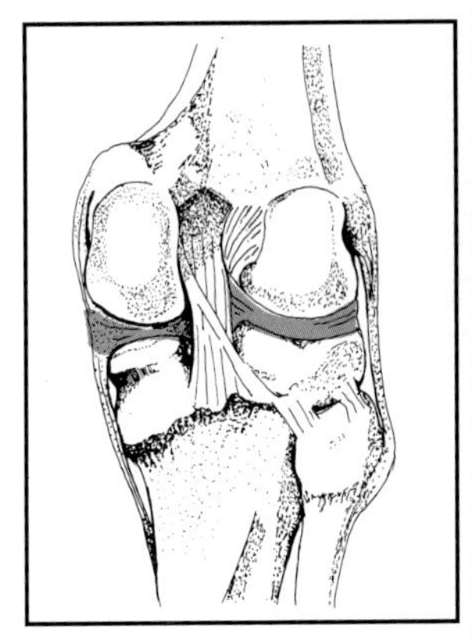

The menisci on the inner side (medial) and outer side (lateral) are attached to the joint capsule around the outer rim but are free at the thin edge within the joint. They take considerable weight from one bone to the other but unfortunately they regularly get caught within the joint and torn. They are made of a gristly fibrocartilaginous material which has a limited capacity to heal so that once torn they tend to remain damaged and usually require removal.

Quadriceps and hamstrings

The menisci and cruciate ligaments can be considered as the static stabilizers of the knee, but just as important are the muscles, the quadriceps at the front and the hamstrings at the back. These act in synchrony taking up and paying out together and appropriate strength of these muscles with the accompanying joint position sense will overcome many of the problems of the inherent instability of the knee.

Patella-femoral joint

The patella or kneecap is the point of attachment for the quadriceps muscles at the front of the thigh and the ligament running from its tip. The patellar ligament attaches on to a bony prominence, the tibial tubercle, at the front of the shin.

The patella is part of the tendon and is not attached to the femur in any other way. Its function is to provide increased leverage for the quadriceps because it moves the

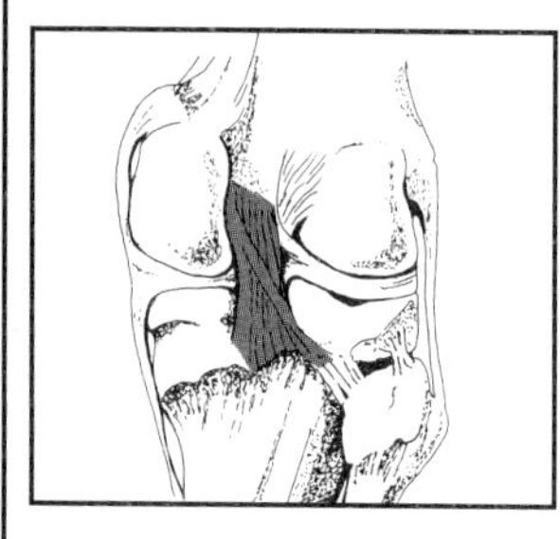

The cruciate ligaments
Two other important structures which improve the stability of the knee by crossing within the joint. The front one, the anterior cruciate ligament, arises from the upper part of the tibia and goes backwards and outwards. It crosses the back ligament which arises from the back of the tibia, coming forwards to insert into the femur. This allows bending and straightening of the knee and yet maintains stability so that the tibia doesn't slip forwards or backwards. Unlike a ball and socket joint there is no inherent stability within the shape of the bone ends. These ligaments, especially the anterior cruciate ligament, are regularly ruptured in sport and can give rise to significant problems of instability. As well as the cruciate ligaments there are two lateral ligaments on either side of the knee which prevent it bending sideways. These are very strong structures but can also be damaged in sporting injuries.

point of movement forwards above the knee. When the knee is fully bent, the patella is in contact with the lower part of the femur and when fully extended is almost completely free of it.

Unfortunately the patella is a site of frequent problems probably due to slight anatomical variations from one person to another and the disorders of patella-femoral movement will be dealt with later.

Calf and ankle

The calf is made up of a group of muscles arranged around the tibia and fibula at the back. These muscles are mainly made up by the bulk of two muscles known as the gastrocnemius and soleus which gives rise to the typical rounded shape. These muscles not only in part span the knee joint as well as the ankle joint (just as the hamstrings above them in the thigh span the hip and the knee) but also help provide a coordinated form of movement throughout the limb.

Muscles of the calf

The calf muscles are matched by anterior tibial muscles at the front of the calf which lift the foot up. These are not surprisingly a lot weaker as all they really need to do is restore the foot's position to a neutral one and maintain ankle stability whereas the calf muscles at the back have to lift the body against gravity in movement. Much like the arrangement in the forearm and hand many of the muscles that move the toes are also situated in the calf and attached to the foot by long tendons. Once again the role of the muscles and tendons crossing the ankle joint is to provide not only movement but also stability.

The ankle joint

The ankle joint itself is a synovial hinge type joint. It is made up of the lower parts of the tibia and the inside edge of the lower part of the fibula. They act like a pair of sugar tongs gripping the upper surface of the upper bone of the foot (the talus) to bend it upwards and downwards. These are the only movements possible at the ankle joint and strong inside and outside ligaments support the joint and prevent side to side movement. These ligaments are commonly injured in a sprained ankle.

Below the ankle joint is the subtalar joint which moves in the opposite direction, side to side, and this means that a universal joint action very similar to that in a car occurs between the shin bone and the heel bone. The heel can be rotated round in a circle, backwards and forwards at the ankle, side to side at the subtalar joint.

In front of the subtalar joint but still in the hind foot there are the mid-tarsal joints. These allow the front part of the foot to twist on the back part.

The whole combination of these three hind foot joints, the ankle, subtalar and mid-tarsal complex, give rise to a highly mobile arrangement which allows you to negotiate rough terrain and always have some part of the foot in contact with the ground.

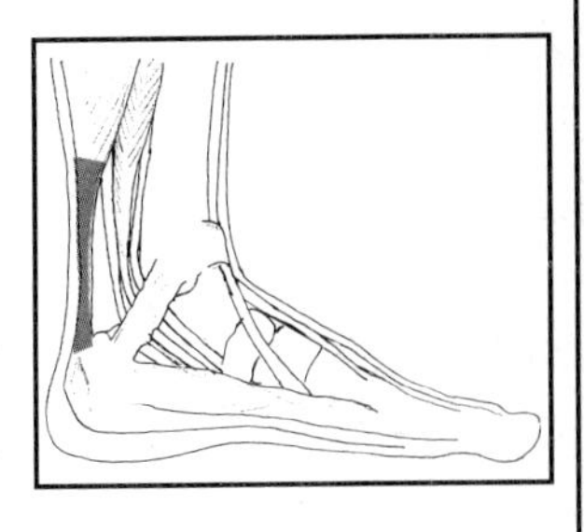

The achilles' tendon
The calf muscles are inserted into the achilles' tendon which is attached to the back of the heel. Once again this is a prominent spur projecting out from behind the point of movement of the ankle that provides a very strong lever for action. The calf muscles at the back pull the heel bone up pushing the foot down and this is critical in running, sprinting and jumping.

Foot

The anatomy of the foot is remarkably similar to that in the hand - the same sorts of numbers of bones, the same arrangements and in some cases the same names. However, the functions could hardly be more different.

Although we no longer need our feet as prehensile objects like our arboreal ancestors did, there are still layers of small muscles within the foot which have the potential for fairly fine movement of the toes although this is rarely necessary in day to day activity. The normal posture and position of the toes and foot relies very heavily on these intrinsic muscles and if they are allowed to waste away with disuse, a rather flattened foot with curly toes can ensue which can be a cause of pain. Exercises for the intrinsic muscles can often prevent or relieve this problem.

Fitness

• ***Cardiovascular fitness***
The increased efficiency of your heart and lungs to get the oxygen into your body and pump it round to the muscles that need it. A fit person can run at a steady rate for many miles and barely get out of breath. An unfit person of the same weight and body strength would be puffing and panting after a few hundred yards. This fitness is achieved without particularly increasing the size of the heart and lungs but just by improving their efficiency. Fit people are as it were turbo charged getting more power without increasing the size of their engine.

• ***Body strength***
This principally means increase in muscle strength but it's also important to remember that ligaments and bones respond to regular exercise and increase in strength themselves. This is becoming increasingly important in the prevention of osteoporosis (senile brittle bones).

• ***Flexibility***
This is the ability to put your joints through their full range of movement. Unless you do this regularly they are inclined to stiffen up. This reduces your overall mobility and also increases the risk of damage to tendons and muscles if you are over stretched.

We often hear people saying they are fit or unfit or in shape but what do we actually mean by this term, fit for what exactly? In the broadest sense, fitness is the ability to undertake physical activity. The human body is capable of a very impressive range of physical activity as witnessed at one extreme by the performance of Olympic athletes. With appropriate training this ability extends, albeit to a lesser extent, into old age and is certainly not confined to very young people. The vast majority of us, however, are not particularly anxious to regularly undertake high level physical activity and most people in the modern civilized world lead a very sedentary existence.

The important principle to grasp, however, is that our ability to perform our relatively limited activity and to avoid injury while doing it is greatly enhanced if we are fit enough to undertake slightly more than we need. A good analogy of this is the car. It is often said that there is little point in buying a car that can greatly exceed the national speed limit as you can never enjoy its full potential. However, although you may never need to travel at 120 miles per hour a car able to do so will be able to cruise much more comfortably at 70 miles per hour than one with a top speed of 70 miles per hour. Similarly a larger capacity, more powerful engine is going to have a much greater lifetime and is less likely to be overtaxed in normal use with less chance of breakdown than a small engined car working at maximum pitch.

The great bonus with your body is that rather than having to buy a more powerful engine you can tune up the one you already have to provide this extra capacity, the disadvantage is that you have to keep tuning it up in the form of regular exercise otherwise it will revert back to its original form.

Three elements of fitness

These are cardiovascular fitness, body strength and flexibility as defined in the column on the left. Clearly, sports people will develop one particular area of physical fitness to suit their particular sport. A marathon runner will have great cardiovascular fitness, a weight lifter great body strength and a gymnast great mobility. But all of them need to concentrate on the other aspects as well to some extent and for non-sports people who just want to be in good shape some elements of all three are essential to be fit and healthy. The latter part of this chapter outlines an exercise programme which should maintain these aspects of fitness with a simple regular workout.

Normal response to exercise

Before we can understand what fitness is, we need to understand the body's mechanism for coping with physical exercise and thus how we can improve it. Exercise means increased physical activity which means increased muscle activity in particular as well as increased strain on the bones, tendons, ligaments and joints.

As has already been mentioned muscle contraction requires a huge amount of energy and this energy demand increases rapidly with increased activity. To provide this energy the chemical processes within the muscle cells have to work faster and in order to do so they need more raw materials in the form of glucose and oxygen.

The main waste product from this activity is carbon dioxide. The muscles get the oxygen and glucose via the bloodstream and excrete the carbon dioxide via the same method. It follows that they must require much greater blood flow during activity. This increased blood flow to the muscles occurs in two separate ways. The heart increases the blood flow throughout the body and secondly more of that flow is diverted to the muscles and away from areas such as the gut.

Increased blood flow
The heart does this in two ways:
- *It increases the number of beats a minute*
- *It increases the amount of blood it pumps per beat.*

At rest the heart is pumping five litres a minute but during exercise this can go up five fold to 25 litres a minute. The blood is diverted to the muscles by blood vessels clamping down to areas such as the gut and opening up within the muscles themselves.

Adrenaline and the sympathetic nervous system

All the changes described above are effected by two associated systems in the body. The first is a special system of nerves running throughout the body called the sympathetic nervous system. These nerves travel to the blood vessels, the heart and the skin. This nervous system is backed up by a hormone, adrenaline which is produced by the second associated system, the adrenal glands which lie above both kidneys. In response to nervous impulses from the brain, adrenaline is produced into the blood stream which has a similar effect as the sympathetic nervous system.

In anticipation of exercise or some other performance or confrontation, your brain will activate these two systems and you will experience that familiar sensation of butterflies in the stomach, thumping heart and sticky palms. All too often in the modern world this reaction occurs as a result of some impending interview, public speaking engagement or argument but what your body is actually doing is getting itself ready to take physical exercise such as running away or fighting. It is thought that regularly frustrating the system without giving it the benefit of making use of this preparation in the form of violent exercise and blowing off steam may give rise to problems such as high blood pressure.

Other responses to exercise

One of the by-products of the chemical reactions needed to produce energy for active muscle is heat and this has to be lost again to stop the blood temperature from rising dramatically. Because we are warm blooded creatures we cannot tolerate any significant lowering or raising of our body temperature. We therefore have very subtle and intricate mechanisms for controlling our temperature.

Temperature loss

The most obvious way of losing heat is to sweat. The water produced on the skin evaporates and cools us and at the same time, if necessary, the blood vessels to the surface of the skin can open up to increase the skin temperature and thus heat loss. This gives rise to the typical flushed appearance of someone after heavy exercise. These mechanisms are mainly under the control of the sympathetic nervous system once again although there are other factors that play a part.

There is also a slight conflict of interest. On the one hand the main effect of the sympathetic system is to shut down the blood vessels to the skin to divert the blood to the muscles where it is needed most. (This is associated with a degree of sweating for the expected heat loss needed and gives rise to the typical cold, clammy skin you are familiar with associated with the adrenaline response.) However, if heat loss is not sufficient, the blood vessels in the skin will have to open up to get more hot blood near the surface of the body to lose more heat.

Heat is also lost from the lungs, cool air is drawn into them and warm air is blown out. This is a very efficient method especially when the breathing rate goes up and indeed in some animals, such as the dog, it is the only method they have of losing heat as they are unable to sweat. In humans, however, this mechanism is not strictly under the control of the temperature regulation systems and respiratory control is influenced by the level of oxygen and carbon dioxide concentrations within the blood.

Breathing during exercise

Blood is pumped from the heart round the lungs, back to the heart and then round the body. This double cycle takes less than a minute to complete. The red blood cells within the blood stream carry oxygen and carbon dioxide. They pick up the oxygen from the fresh air inhaled into the lungs and carry it around the body, delivering it to the muscles and other organs where it is used to produce energy.

The by-product is carbon dioxide which the red blood cell takes back to the lungs and excretes and the lung breathes out the carbon dioxide into the fresh air again. In order to provide enough oxygen at rest you need to breathe about 12 to 15 times a minute. However, during exercise more oxygen is needed, more carbon dioxide is produced and the respiration rate will go up several times. Once again just like the heart pumping blood, the lungs can increase the amount of air available to your blood not only by increasing the respiratory rate but also the depth and therefore the size of your breath. Respiratory rate is under the control of chemical receptors within the blood system which detects the concentration of gases particularly carbon dioxide circulating. If the carbon dioxide level goes up the respiratory rate increases so that more is blown off from the lungs and the level returns to normal. The rate

Weight loss
Although increased exercise will burn up more glucose and this can be of help in weight control it certainly isn't enough in its own right. If you want to lose weight, an exercise regime must go hand in hand with calorie controlled eating.

then goes back to its resting level. This is the typical feedback system for body control.

Food and exercise

Up until now we have concentrated on the requirements of getting oxygen to the active muscle but of course the chemical process also needs raw materials of food in the form of glucose.

Glucose

Glucose is a small sugar molecule which is the basic building block of most other sugars. The body can create it from any form of carbohydrate and indeed other constituents of the diet, but most of it comes from carbohydrates within the diet. It is impossible for the gut to continue to create glucose at the rate it is needed for exercise; therefore, the body stores glucose ready for use in the liver in the form of a compact starch known as glycogen. This is readily broken down to produce the glucose as necessary.

The glycogen store in the liver will last about 24 hours with normal activity and therefore clearly needs to be regularly topped up with meals. If you are able to eat regular meals and allow a period of rest afterwards for the process of digestion, these glycogen stores will be kept full and the value of glucose drinks or tablets is unlikely to provide any greater benefit. Certainly it is unnecessary, unhelpful and potentially hazardous to eat or drink a lot while or just before taking vigorous exercise.

Aerobic and anaerobic exercise

Before moving on to how regular exercise can improve fitness, i.e. how one can improve the efficiency of all the above responses to activity, it is important to understand a bit more about the chemical reactions that take place in the muscle during exercise.

Both the chemical pathways described in the column on the right are in action in the normal exercising individual to some extent, but by taking different forms of exercise you can make your muscles use one system more than the other. As far as the muscle is concerned, it is only interested in getting enough energy but the effect of concentrating on one set of exercises (and thus chemical reactions).

The energy released by both these reactions goes to charge up a chemical battery. This is called ATP. It is not used up in any chemical reaction but provides the muscle fibres with immediate energy when it is needed. It releases its energy and converts to ADP and is then ready for recharging. All this energy production is being done in small intracellular capsules called mitochondria with which muscle cells are loaded.

How fitness occurs

Even if you are grossly unfit the body's normal responses to exercise (which have been outlined earlier) still act, but in a very inefficient way. If an unfit person runs for a bus, the pulse rate will increase, the blood supply down to the gut will shut down, the blood circulation to the muscles will open up and he or she will start panting. However, it is likely that this unfit person will never reach the bus. He or she will have to stop short with muscles aching and with painful gasps of breath.

The same individual, after tuning these same responses for a few months, will be able to make the bus with a few bounds, not out of breath and with only a few beads of sweat on the brow, feeling a great deal better for it.

Your active body has all these potentials, so how can you tune them up? You can improve the efficiency of all these complex responses using a very simple principle - by gently increasing the demands on your body it will respond by becoming better at meeting those demands.

Two other important principles must also be noted. The emphasis must be on gentle build up. A violent attempt to knock your body into shape will fail and cause more damage than good. Secondly the process needs to be continued and regular otherwise your body will revert back to its original form. This does not mean you need to be a fitness fanatic to be in better shape, but you do need

• *Aerobic*
The term aerobic has now become popular to describe a form of exercises popularized by Jane Fonda and others but actually the word describes a specific biochemical set of reactions. Aerobic literally means with air and anaerobic means without air. By air we mean oxygen.

• *Anaerobic*
Chemical reactions which make energy need oxygen but during its temporary absence in prolonged or violent exercise, there are mechanisms by which the energy can be produced without a free supply of oxygen. This is a less efficient method and for any individual molecule of glucose used in this method, less energy is produced. However, it is a good back up system and is important when extra energy is required or where stamina is needed for prolonged muscle use. This secondary system is the anaerobic system.

Body's response to increased demand

An example of the way the body can respond has an analogy with skin thickening or callus formation. If you use, let's say, a pick-axe all day in your work, your body will respond by building up thick calluses on the palms of your hands to protect your skin. These would disappear very quickly if you stopped the activity. Similarly if you have soft hands and went at the use of a pick-axe like a bull at a gate one weekend you would almost certainly develop blisters. You would be worse off and unable to continue with the job in hand. In this instance your body has not been given time to respond to its new demands and you've overloaded the skin and it has failed but if you built up use gradually you would be able to develop well-calloused palms and happily swing your pick-axe for hours on end without disturbing the skin.

to make some time available throughout the week for a regular programme of exercise.

Improving cardiovascular fitness

This is what most people mean by being generally fit. It is also known as cardiovascular conditioning. Fitness in this respect means an increased ability to provide your body, and in particular your muscles, with oxygen. The minimum requirement of oxygen is the same for fit and unfit people, about 3 cc per kilogram per minute, but the oxygen provision can be greatly enhanced. The fit person does this in the following way.

Heart output

This is increased, not by increasing the heart rate, but by increasing the amount of blood the heart pumps in each beat. In the fit person the heart will empty more completely and whereas in the normal individual 70 cc of blood is pumped per beat this can go up over a hundred in the fit person. This significant increase in cardiac output means the heart can beat relatively less quickly which in fact makes it more efficient and allows it greater recovery time between beats.

One of the easiest ways to test cardiovascular fitness is the heart rate, both at rest and at effort. The normal resting pulse rate of an adult is between 70 and 80. This can drop down to between 60 and 70 in a fit person and a great deal lower in exceptional circumstances.

Composition of the blood

Not only does the cardiac output increase but the blood volume, i.e. the amount of blood in the body and the concentration of red cells within it, both go up which improves the capacity of the body to carry oxygen to the tissues and carbon dioxide away from them.

This improved oxygen transfer reduces the build up of blood carbon dioxide, replacing the rapid respiration and gasping of the unfit person with long deep breaths which achieves a more efficient transfer of gas in the lungs than short sharp gasps where oxygen does not have a chance to get right down into the lungs.

Blood distribution

This pattern is also improved in the fit person. This is particularly noticeable in the ability to lose extra heat. The fit person will appear to sweat much more readily which will lose heat more rapidly albeit with a rapid loss of fluid. This allows the body to get rid of a lot more heat without resorting to skin flushing which as has been mentioned earlier, is a contradictory reaction as it diverts blood away from the important muscle areas. This is readily observed by watching amateur joggers. The fit people have normal coloration but will be sweating heavily. The unfit will be glowing bright red in the face and looking distinctly less cool in every sense of the word.

The following are examples of good general aerobic exercising which have been estimated as making the equivalent oxygen demand on the body:

- *Running one mile in 8 minutes.*
- *Swimming for 15 minutes.*
- *Cycling for 5 miles or 20 minutes.*
- *Playing tennis for 35 minutes.*

Improving your fitness

Broadly speaking in order to gain the benefits of this fitness you need to make your muscles ask for more oxygen from time to time to improve your body's ability to provide it. This, of course, means taking regular aerobic exercise. It does not necessarily mean doing 'aerobic exercises' as offered by classes up and down the country (although this of course would be a perfectly good way of doing it). It does mean taking any exercise which uses a large quantity of your muscle groups for a reasonable period of time without exhausting them so that they produce muscle energy by aerobic rather than the anaerobic mechanism.

You will notice that all of the activities listed in the right hand column involve most of the major muscle groups in the body and thus make generous demands for oxygen provision. These examples illustrate the rough equivalent value and may help you to choose different patterns of aerobic exercise you may want to build in to your regular routine. They are not necessarily the right level of exercise to start with if you are very unfit and of course they're not individually in any way essential to a

Fit for fitness
As with all other fitness regimes the two golden rules apply for cardiovascular fitness, namely your routine must be regular and your build up of activity gradual. There is a great temptation when starting to rush into it with initial enthusiasm, running too far for too long and exhausting yourself. You may possibly injure yourself in the process without any benefit. This is more likely to put you off than do any good at all.

good fitness programme. What is clear, however, is that running is the most efficient way of taking aerobic exercise and this, combined with its lack of any need for special equipment, is the major reason why it is such a popular form of exercise today.

Whether you just want to stay in shape and feel fit and healthy or you are training for a particular sport some form of aerobic exercise to improve cardiovascular fitness is essential.

Building up fitness

If you build up activities gradually and make a regular commitment to it you will be rewarded by steady but noticeable improvement in your ability. For example, if you take up running as your main form of aerobic exercise you can start by working out a course of approximately a mile, set off on this, jogging gently until you become out of breath. This will happen quite quickly if you are unfit and you will note your heart pounding within a few hundred yards. As soon as you are unable to hold a conversation while running due to breathlessness slow down to a fast walking pace to get your breath back. As soon as this has happened you can get back to running. You will be able to achieve this relatively comfortably.

Within the first few sessions you will notice no significant difference but you can be sure that the signs of increased heart rate and respiration rate are telling your cardiovascular system that they must be more efficient in providing your muscles with oxygen. In due course you will find that you are walking less and less and running more and more and can gradually build up to running the mile easily without stopping. You can then start increasing the distance. You can obviously use this sort of approach on any aerobic exercise with reference to the rough equivalent values given above.

Endurance

Endurance is the ability of the body to produce prolonged physical activity and for most sports and individuals a degree of endurance is simply achieved by better cardio-vascular fitness as described above.

However, in certain circumstances like marathon running, simply providing enough oxygen efficiently to the muscles is not enough. The individual muscle fibres themselves have to have the ability of being able to continue to produce work for prolonged periods. To some extent individual muscle fibres can rest while others take over in an active muscle which helps it to continue producing regular contractions but the individual person's make up of muscle is also important. There are two forms of muscle fibre, one suited for fast response and bursts of high energy and activity, and the other suited to slow endurance-type activity. In some creatures like the pigeon these two fibres are grouped within different muscles so that in the pigeon's breast it has a muscle on either side for fast bursts of wing beat and another muscle next to it for the slow regular beat needed for long flying journeys. In humans these two fibres are mixed within each muscle group and the quantity of fibres in any individual's muscle is genetically determined and therefore cannot be changed. This means that some people are more suited to endurance activities and will make better marathon runners, and other people more suited for fast activities such as sprinting. Many other factors including body shape and weight also have an affect. However, to improve endurance, regular prolonged activity is needed to get the best out of your endurance fibres.

Muscle strength

Aerobic exercise uses the muscles to make oxygen demands and improve cardiovascular conditioning but most of these exercises rarely reach the individual muscle's capacity in terms of strength. Marathon runners don't end up with legs the size of body builders. Indeed, often they appear to be quite the opposite and yet these legs can carry them at a fast running pace for over 20 miles.

In order to increase muscle strength and muscle size the muscle needs to be used to its maximum limit of strength so that the body will respond by making it

Circuit training
For each particular muscle group, the first thing you need to do is work out what the maximum weight is you can lift or push with that particular muscle. You lift increasing weights until you reach this maximum level at which point the muscle will start to shake and ultimately you'll be unable to lift a weight beyond a certain level.

Once this maximum is defined your subsequent exercises are done on the basis of a percentage of this weight and the exercises are repeated a number of times with this lower weight. In general terms if you are building muscle for bulk and strength you do a small number of repetitions with a larger percentage of the maximum weight and if you are building up muscles for endurance you do a larger number of repetitions for a smaller percentage. An example might be 85% of maximum weight for eight repetitions or 65% for 12 repetitions.

stronger and this involves some form of resistive exercise, i.e. lifting, pulling or pushing weights or springs.

Muscle bulk

Muscles become stronger by increasing the size of the individual muscle fibres rather than making more of them. This increase in size or hypertrophy gives rise to increased muscle bulk so prized by the body builder. It is a myth that these body builders' muscles are weak. They may not have much endurance but they are certainly as strong as they look. In muscle strength exercises individual muscle groups are singled out for isolated work. This is of more importance for individual sports or for body building and in these circumstances a detailed understanding of the anatomy and function of each muscle is needed so that the appropriate exercises can be done. However, for someone just wanting to build up a good general muscle shape they can be less specific and concentrate on general groups for resistive exercises, e.g. press-ups which exercise more than one specific muscle but are resistive exercises designed to build up muscle strength and bulk.

Equipment

A whole generation of complicated machinery has been developed and is now available for muscle strength exercise. These range from bar bells to complex machines like the Nautilus. These latter machines certainly make it easier to isolate a muscle for exercise and perform the exercise correctly and safely, but they are not necessary and as long as the basic principles are understood the barest minimum of equipment is needed for a good work-out routine.

Circuit training

When planning an exercise programme for muscle strength you can work out depending on your goals which muscle groups you choose to exercise and build up. The resistive exercises are then undertaken in a set circuit. This circuit of exercises may be repeated two or three times in a session.

If you are serious about body building you are strongly advised to go to a professional gym where not only will good equipment be available but also you will have the benefit of professional advice working out a programme to suit yourself and start doing the exercises under proper supervision. However, the two golden rules of fitness training apply to this as with everything else. Your exercises need to be on a regular basis and the start needs to be gradual.

Flexibility

This is the third of our main components of general fitness. It's often suggested that the ability to touch your toes is a sign that you are fit but why is it important in an active person?

There are two main reasons. Firstly, if your joints can't be put through their full range of movement, then clearly the function of that joint will be reduced by the relevant amount and ultimately your activity (be it sport or day to day life) will also be reduced. Secondly, and possibly most importantly, with increased cardiovascular fitness and muscle strength you will have much greater power going through the joint and trying to put it through its full range of movements. If the ligaments and joint capsule are stiff they and the surrounding tissues can get damaged. It is therefore vital to have a good stretch-out routine before taking exercise.

Variability

There is a great natural variability in joint flexibility. Joint stiffness comes from supporting structures of the joint, particularly the ligaments and capsule, but also the muscles. At one end of the normal spectrum are people who are hypermobile or 'double-jointed'. In fact, they don't have any more joints than anyone else and indeed their joints themselves are quite normal to examination and X-ray. It is the muscles, tendons and ligaments that are loose.

Stretching

Being very hypermobile is probably a disadvantage and although some sporting activities such as gymnastics might be enhanced to some extent, hypermobility of a dramatic nature can lead to early joint degeneration.

However, in the majority of cases, the unfit person is rather stiffer than is good for him or her and some regular stretching routine should be included in your exercise programme. Once again the principle is simple, improving flexibility is achieved by gently stretching the stiffer joints and muscles on a regular basis. It is important not to force or bounce on these stiff areas in the hope of speeding up the process as you will inevitably injure yourself. But if you are persistent and regular with your exercises you will soon be rewarded by an increase in mobility. Which particular joint group and how far you stretch them very much depends on what you want from your body. Ballet dancers will need more flexibility than muscle builders but the latter group must do some stretching routine nevertheless.

Increasing your pulse rate

The essence of warming up is first to switch on the body's exercise response by taking acrobic exercise in the form of light jogging or running on the spot for a few minutes to get the pulse rate up and the blood vessels opened up to the muscle groups. Your heart will increase its output and your muscles will warm up.

In sports such as football this aerobic exercise can be combined with kicking the ball around and getting your eye in and this process also probably helps to tune up your joint position sense and prepare your legs for the stretches and strains that they'll have to endure in the game.

Before other sports, such as tennis, make sure that when you're knocking up you do run around and warm up in this respect rather than stand on the back line just knocking the ball back and forth. What you are trying to avoid is having to make your body respond to violent surges of exercise without having given it adequate preparation.

Warming-up routines

Whether you are super fit or not you will still need to prepare yourself before any particular activity and this is called warming up or limbering up. It is simply a matter of winding up the body to be prepared for activity to improve your performance and more particularly reduce injury. In this latter respect many amateur sports injuries could be avoided with a proper warm-up routine. Even if you aren't a sportsperson and are just going out to do some vigorous gardening, there is still a lot to be said for turning on your body's activity mechanisms and, as it were, putting yourself into high gear.

Warm-up stretches

Once the body is warmed up after a few minutes of this activity and your pulse rate has gone up from the resting position by 10 or 20 beats a minute, you can then do some stretching exercises. These should not be done with the muscles 'cold' as they will be stiffer and injury more likely. The particular stretching exercises will obviously relate to the sort of activity you are about to embark on and some general examples are given below but you'll all be familiar with this limbering up routine on the professional sportsfield before a soccer match. Here stretches are particularly aimed at making sure the quadriceps and hamstring muscles are fully stretched out as ruptures in these muscles during high activity are not uncommon.

Fitness and health

All this information about getting fit presupposes that your body can respond to the extra demands that activity makes on it, but, of course, this is not true if you are ill.

Heart and lung disease

There are not many diseases or disorders that reduce your ability to build muscle strength or gain flexibility but there are many common diseases and problems that prevent cardiovascular conditioning.

Balanced exercise programme

All these elements of fitness will be needed in different quantities and proportions depending on what you want to get out of your active body: body builders will go for strength; long distance runners for aerobic fitness and endurance; gymnasts for mobility; and they will all need the other elements in a lesser degree.

Some sports, in particular swimming, seem to combine all three in a relatively even proportion. This is one of the reasons why it is such a popular activity and is regularly recommended by doctors as a good, safe, all round way of keeping fit. In terms of looking good too the physique of the male and female swimmer is often very much the sort of shape that we regard as healthy and fit finding the over-developed physique of the body builder more of a fascination than an attraction.

Seek medical advice

If you want to improve your fitness, and there are any doubts about your health, you will need proper medical supervision before embarking on it. Hopefully, if you are under the care of your doctor, he or she will have already given you a sensible exercise programme to make the most of your condition, but if not go and ask for one.

If you haven't been particularly unwell but are very unfit, possibly overweight and have smoked or are still smoking, it is worthwhile seeking medical advice and a quick check-up before embarking on a regular exercise programme if you are in your late thirties or over as heart attacks become increasingly common at this stage.

Heart and lung disease are the commonest in our Western society and the commonest causes of death. In Great Britain in particular there is an appalling record of cardiovascular disease in the form of atherosclerosis (hardening and narrowing of the arteries) which leads to myocardial infarction (heart attack). This is principally due to the fat laden diet and smoking. In coronary artery disease the arteries that supply the heart itself, clog up and reduce the amount of oxygen that can be brought to the heart muscle. This reduces the heart's ability to respond to exercise by increasing its output and if a great demand is made of it this occasionally can be disastrous as areas of ischaemia (lack of blood) can occur in the heart muscle and a heart attack ensue. The scenario of an overweight business man running for a train after a big meal and collapsing dead with a heart attack is a familiar one to us. Chest disease in the form of bronchitis will also reduce the ability to get fit because it reduces the body's ability to increase its oxygen intake which is an important part of cardiovascular conditioning.

Asthma, a common condition in childhood, can also reduce the ability to get fit but it can be controlled . There are many famous top level professional athletes who suffer from this condition who, with appropriate control, have gone on to lead a very full and active life.

Smoking and fitness

The title of this section is of course a contradiction in terms. Smoking and fitness are complete opposites. Response to smoking is almost exactly the opposite to what you are trying to achieve when you become fit, and although most people are quite bored of being told how damaging smoking can be, the point needs to be made quite clearly nevertheless.

To go into detail about all the detrimental effects that cigarette smoking has would take a book as long as the whole of this one, but suffice it to say that since the original discovery linking smoking with lung cancer even that enormous and significant discovery has paled into insignificance next to our understanding of the detrimental effect it has on other heart and lung conditions of a much more common nature, notably cardiovascular disease.

Oxygen reduction

One of the most immediate effects of cigarette smoking is to reduce the level of available oxygen to the body tissues - exactly the opposite to what we are trying to achieve with cardiovascular conditioning. The way that smoking does this is several-fold. First it causes constriction of the airways in the lungs as well as irritation. This reduces the lung efficiency. Secondly, once the carbon monoxide from the smoke gets into the bloodstream, it blocks the red blood cells' capacity to take oxygen. The body responds to this by making more blood cells but this just makes the blood rather thicker and this in turn can reduce its efficacy in transmitting oxygen to the tissues. Thirdly cigarette smoking has a direct effect on the blood vessels making them clamp down. Once again this is the direct opposite of what one is trying to achieve in cardiovascular fitness and if all this wasn't enough the nicotine in the smoke actually stimulates the heart to try and beat faster. You might think that this would have a beneficial effect in overcoming some of these problems but the heart has got to do more work with a reduced level of oxygen and this puts considerable strain on it.

It's very easy to see that smoking has a devastating effect on any attempt to improve your cardiovascular conditioning. The good news for smokers however is that it's never too late to stop. Certainly in the young person all of these changes are completely reversible and most of them are in the older person as well although some residual blood vessel stiffness from the arterial disease may persist.

It's also impossible and indeed foolhardy to try and offset the disadvantages of smoking by taking regular exercise. You can't expect your body to give better performance if you are continually poisoning it. Unfortunately, there is no way round the problem. You either give up smoking or give up the idea of having a healthy, active body.

Calorie intake
A normal person will require up to about 2000 calories of energy per day and this is principally provided in the diet by fats and carbohydrates. The exact requirements will depend on your day-to-day activity, age, sex and size. However, this can go up significantly to 5000 or 6000 calories a day if you are regularly involved in hard exercise or manual work. This can still be provided by a normal healthy diet, high in energy rich foods but some people like to supplement it in certain activities with high energy glucose drinks. It is important to realize that the term energy here is slightly misleading. Taking large quantities of glucose provides calories for your active body, it won't of course pep you up or in any way improve your general fitness and a few gulps of fizzy glucose drink immediately before violent exercise is more likely to slow you up rather than speed you up.

The message therefore is a healthy diet at regular mealtimes and allowing an hour or two of digestion time after your meal before exercise.

Fitness, food and rest

A healthy, balanced diet is essential for health and fitness. It needs to contain the three main elements of a diet, carbohydrate, protein and fat but with low amounts of saturated animal fat which is bad for the cardiovascular system. You should take in adequate quantities of fibre or roughage for normal bowel activity and the trace elements and vitamins are also needed. In a proper diet there is no indication that the healthy fit person needs vitamin supplements. There are circumstances such as in babyhood and pregnancy when extra vitamins are valuable but if your diet is chosen appropriately there is no evidence that increased vitamin intake in the form of supplements gives any benefit to the active person, nor improves sporting performance.

Fitness and rest

We have concentrated on activity and exercise but of course it is just as important to allow your body to recover after activity and rest properly. Even in the most strenuous work-out routines for the professional athlete there is little advantage in training over five times a week. This is much less of a problem in the ordinary individual who is interested in staying in shape but if you are going to embark on an intensive fitness programme, do build in adequate rest days and times to allow your body to recover adequately.

Fitness and fatness

People who are overweight already know about the importance of calorie control and reducing calorie intake to below your necessary requirements to lose weight. It is outside the scope of this book to deal with calorie controlled diets and weight loss but one or two important principles need to be made clear.

It is possible to be slightly overweight and in good physical condition with improved cardiovascular fitness, strength and flexibility. If you are mildly overweight, i.e. 10% or 15%, or roughly speaking a stone above your ideal weight, there is nothing to stop you building up your activity gradually as outlined above. Indeed, you will probably find that it should be easier to control your weight if you do build up cardiovascular fitness, endurance and muscle strength.

However, if you are greatly overweight you've really got to address the weight problem before you can tackle your fitness. Increased exertion carrying a lot of extra weight can be hazardous and to achieve increased aerobic activity may be quite difficult although swimming is valuable in this respect as your body weight will be supported while you take your exercise. Once your weight starts coming down you can build up your activity .

It is a fallacy to think that exercise alone will be the answer to overweight problems. It's certainly part of it but not all of it and you can't divorce being overweight from the laws of thermodynamics, i.e. your desire to lose weight has got to be greater than your desire to eat and some form of calorie control is critical. Having said that, don't be too harsh with your calorie control to start with if you are combining it with an exercise programme. Your body taking more activity will need more calories and common sense must prevail. Certainly you should not embark on calorie control diets of less than a thousand calories for a man and 800 for a woman per day without proper medical supervision. You should avoid fad diets and starvation diets and concentrate on understanding dietary control and changing your lifetime eating patterns. Taking on a diet is like taking on a dog, it's for life not for Christmas. All the successful diet and weight loss programmes involve some behavioural and eating habit changes rather than simply relying on changes of recipes.

Fitness and age

There are two important aspects here, fitness in children and fitness with advancing years. Broadly speaking it's possible to improve the three key elements of physical fitness at any age from childhood to old age but there are one or two specific provisos and these need to be understood.

Summary

Normal activity of aerobic exercise is enough to keep children healthy enough to compete at school level in sports and enjoy normal activity. There is an increasing demand on young children to perform at a higher and higher level because of the pressure of competition nowadays. While this may have benefits for the individual sport and the country for which they may compete in terms of the high standards of excellence that can be achieved, it may be at the expense of doing long term damage. While it is easy to be impressed by the ability of some 13-year-old gymnasts at the Olympic Games, these children often pay a very high physical and psychological price for their success. It behoves trainers, teachers and parents to guard against over-zealous training of young people.

Children and fitness

To some extent children are naturally fit and that's probably because they are naturally active. If you see children at a school playground 'at rest' very few of them will be standing still. If you see adults at rest they will be sitting or standing. Most children therefore are undertaking quite a lot of aerobic exercise from day to day and in general are in good cardiovascular condition. For the vast majority of sports and activities they need to enjoy there is no particular need to concentrate too hard on improving this.

From the strength point of view there is a limit to how strong their muscles will build which is principally under hormonal influence. The male sex hormone, testosterone, is needed for large body building which is why men can build massive muscles and women can't. Children too do not have any male sex hormone and will not be able to build big muscles. Some children are naturally endowed with fairly large muscles and others aren't, but apart from normal activity it is unwise to encourage too much resistive training in the form of circuit weights before the onset of puberty. Indeed in the growing skeleton where there are naturally weak areas at the insertion of some major tendons and at the growing ends of the bones, these exercises can be very detrimental causing pain and disability.

Children are also naturally flexible. Their ligaments, muscles and tendons are healthy and contain a greater proportion of an elastic material than adults. Little is needed in the form of stretching exercises in the healthy child and once again over exertion in this respect is more likely to do damage than good.

Fitness and increasing age

You are never too old to have an active body but there are two aspects of increasing age which need to be understood. First of all there are one or two normal changes that occur as we grow older that are inclined to reduce our ability to achieve such high levels of fitness. These alone, however, are not enough to stop seventy- or eighty-year-olds still enjoying an active life and sport.

The second problem is greater. Increasing age makes

us more prone to various diseases and disorders which reduce our ability to get fit or make it hazardous to try. The next section deals with the common disorders that affect the skeleton, many of which are age related, and discusses those individual points there. However, we will end this section on fitness by looking at the normal changes that occur to our active body as we grow older.

Normal changes

One or two general changes affect our bodies as we get older and this reflects on the individual aspects of fitness. The first is that we become slightly weaker, not simply from the muscular strength point of view but also our bones, tendons and ligaments all are slightly weaker compared to a young adult or child. This is partly due to the fact that the repair and reparative process that occurs in all tissues is slightly turned down with increasing age. Wear and tear on our bodies takes its toll and is less rapidly and enthusiastically repaired by the cells of the body.

As well as being slightly slower and more inefficient in their task, the body cells don't produce the same quality materials that they used to in their youth. The collagen and matrix proteins are not quite the same and this affects strength and flexibility. Collagen fibres are the strong body's equivalent of steel cables that support the ligaments, bones and cartilage but mixed with these in the child's tissues are elastin fibres, not stiff like collagen but bendy and rubbery. These elastin fibres are lost with age and wear and tear. In the skin this loss of elasticity gives rise to the typical wrinkles of old age. The skin no longer springs back to its original position when stretched and wrinkles form. These general effects take their toll on the individual aspects of fitness because the older person tends to be generally stiffer not only in the joints but in the blood vessels as well.

The cardiovascular system

This is less able to respond to vigorous exercise, the heart beats less powerfully, empties less completely and the blood vessels, being somewhat stiffer, don't open up so

Is fitness bad for me?
The major risk of physical fitness is that in trying to achieve it too enthusiastically, you break the two cardinal rules of gradual and regular exercise and over exert yourself too soon causing an injury. Although you will probably make a good recovery from any injury sustained, it may put you off from ever trying to become fit again.

If you have been very fit and then stop activity out of choice or illness, your body will slowly revert to its former state. The speed at which it does this depends on the type of fitness. Broadly speaking, cardiovascular fitness will wane fairly rapidly over several weeks, muscular strength will go off over a period of some months and flexibility gained in youth may persist for several years without particular attempts to maintain it. If you have been very strong it's untrue that your muscles turn to fat if you no longer use them. You may indeed tend to put on weight with reduced activity but this has probably got more to do with eating habits and reduced aerobic activity than with any complex change in biochemistry.

fully nor do the other blood vessels in the body shut down so tight. This has the effect of reducing the capacity of the body to increase oxygen provision.

Muscle strength and endurance

This is also reduced somewhat. In response to resistive exercises the muscles will enlarge in old age but will never achieve the generous rounded proportions of the younger person. Muscle endurance, however, does survive longer than some other aspects of fitness as witnessed by the fact that many marathon runners remain competitive for a much greater age than the sprinting sportsman.

Flexibility

This is affected and the older person tends to become stiffer and certainly less elastic. However, it is an area which can be improved with stretching and certainly gentle stretching routines are important in a fitness programme in the elderly.

Although these changes do exist, the fact remains that if they have good health most elderly people can be a great deal fitter than they are. This will not only make their lives more enjoyable and rewarding but will also reduce ill health and the risk of injury.

	Lungs and heart *Walk or jog on spot pulling arms forward and backwards in a rowing action. Alternate with flexing the arm up to the shoulder and back.*	***Waist, back, shoulders*** *Feet apart, knees slightly bent, fingertips behind ears. Twist to left, hold for 5 counts; repeat to right.*	***Shoulders, hips, knees*** *Feet apart, hands on head. Squat down as far as comfortable. Stretch up straight on tiptoes pushing arm above head.*	***Waist and thighs*** *Lie on one side, hand supporting head. Bend bottom leg. Hold other leg 6" from ground, raise to 2 feet up, hold for 5 counts, lower slowly to 6".*	***Waist, stomach*** *Lie on back, fingertips behind ears. Bend alternate knees to chest, other leg off floor. Touch opposite elbow to knee. Raise shoulders as strength increases.*	***Buttocks, thighs*** *Kneel. Flex knee to chest, lower forehead to knee. Slowly straighten leg out, gently straighten neck, hold for 5 counts. Repeat with other leg.*
20-30	80	14	20	25	20	30
4 weeks	300	30	50	50	90	50
30-40	50	12	18	20	20	20
6 weeks	300	30	40	50	70	50
40-50	50	10	15	15	15	15
6 weeks	250	25	30	35	50	35
50-60	40	10	12	10	10	10
4 weeks	200	20	20	30	30	30
60-70	40	8	8	5	10	8
6 weeks	150	20	15	20	25	20

Find your age group in the left-hand column. For each exercise, start on the top layer and build up gradually to the repetitions in the lower layer over the number of weeks shown.

Wear loose clothing and training shoes or plimsolls. Floor exercises should be done on a carpet or mat.

The first exercise increases your pulse rate and should leave you slightly out of breath. Repeat it at the end of the programme for greater aerobic fitness.

The flexibility and power exercises which follow should be done smoothly and slowly. Replace any movement which is too difficult or uncomfortable with a similar, less strenuous one. Slow down if you get a cramping feeling in the muscle.

Avoidable conditions

The previous sections have dealt with the normal human anatomy and function of the musculo-skeletal system and introduced the concepts of physical fitness, yet despite the ability of your body to perform incredible feats of strength, agility and speed, the musculo-skeletal system is a common site of problems.

All of us at one time or another will develop problems of a painful and uncomfortable nature somewhere in our musculo-skeletal system. Seen another way round about 30% of a general practitioner's workload will be complaints from patients arising from this aspect of their bodies. Despite this, many of these complaints are truly avoidable with sensible body management. Some may not be completely avoidable but by a sensible approach you can significantly reduce your chance of developing them.

Truly avoidable conditions

This really comprises a group of disorders of overuse or abuse and are usually caused by over-exertion of an unprepared part of the body. Of course, there will always be one or two people who, with all the care in the world, have problems of this nature, but in general it is the domain of the over enthusiastic amateur sportsperson or weekend do-it-yourselfer.

Acute overuse injury

The term 'acute' means there has been a sudden tear or rupture of a substance. It is the opposite to a chronic condition which is discussed later.

Acute injuries can occur in muscles, ligaments and tendons as a result of over exertion on an unwarmed and unstretched body. Occasionally this may occur as the result of a true accident, but more often than not it is just expecting too much too suddenly of an ill-prepared body.

Muscle and tendon ruptures

Acute tears can occur in muscles causing sudden pain, swelling and restriction of movement. This is not uncommon in the quadriceps muscle at the front of the thigh and in the calf.

Tendons can also rupture suddenly, often in slightly older individuals where there may be a bit of age change, but this is regularly compounded with sudden exercise or exertion. A typical site is the achilles' tendon and this may often rupture with a sudden burst of activity such as running for a bus. There is a sudden pain as if someone has struck you in the back of the heel (many squash partners have been falsely accused of assault as a result!). A small defect appears within the tendon which rapidly fills with bruise and you lose the ability to fully push your foot down. The treatment is either plaster or surgical sewing and the recovery takes some months.

When you are lifting a heavy weight keep the back straight, bring the weight in to your centre of gravity so that you aren't leaning over it and use your legs to give the lift not your back muscles as illustrated.

If your job involves a lot of lifting and carrying, don't forget that as time goes on and you get older, possibly fatter and less fit, your ability to lift weights will rapidly wane. Unfortunately, the weights themselves will remain the same. It is therefore essential that you do keep yourself in good shape and regularly reassess your ability to do the tasks expected of you. The more specific problems of back disorder such as slipped disc and chronic back pain are dealt with later.

Acute backstrain

Backache is one of the commonest causes of musculo-skeletal problems and will be dealt with more thoroughly in the next section as there are one or two aspects of it which are not strictly avoidable. However, there is no doubt that the vast majority of people regularly abuse their back and expect more of it than it can perform. Sooner or later bad lifting or carrying techniques will cause an injury.

The exact site of much backache is never discovered but there are one or two conditions where it is likely that either a muscle or ligament within the complex arrangement of the back gets torn simply due to an ill-advised manoeuvre. One of the main problems is lifting and carrying and proper technique is essential if you want to avoid back injury. The diagram illustrates the right way to lift heavy weights. The most important aspect is to make sure that you *can* and indeed *need* to lift the weight in question. In some cases a degree of bravado may be a factor in front of your colleagues or just sheer necessity in the case of an emergency. Nevertheless know what you can lift and under- rather than over-estimate. There are certain weights laid down in many industries which give a good indication of what can be reasonably expected.

Chronic overuse injuries

The term chronic here is used in a proper medical way meaning a prolonged problem rather than implying any severity of injury. These overuse injuries are by far the most common and cover a whole area of sports medicine and annoying musculo-skeletal problems. In general terms they are caused by repetitive use of a single area of the body for longer than it can tolerate. Damage is done but without the dramatic rupture that was described previously. Prolonged inflammation is set up and these problems can often go on for many months and be very troublesome.

Muscle and tendon insertion

One of the commonest sites of such disorders is at the insertion of the muscles or tendons into bone, a site of stress where one tissue type joins another. This build-up of stress causes the local injury. Examples of this include tennis elbow, golfer's elbow and Osgood Schlatter's disease (at the upper end of the shin bone in children). The overuse of tendons can lead to an inflammation in the synovial sheath and this is known as synovitis. Examples of this include achilles' tendinitis and de Quervain's (tenosynovitis of the wrist) and bicipital tendinitis of the shoulder. Chronic overuse of a ligament where it runs over a piece of bone can give rise to inflammation in the underlying fluid-filled friction pad known as the bursa and this gives rise to bursitis as seen as in fascia lata bursitis in middle distance runners. The bone itself can be the subject of overuse injury in the form of fatigue fracture.

Chronic insertion pain

Although this can be a feature of some specific arthritic complaint, it is usually associated with overuse.

Tennis elbow

Tennis elbow is pain which is localized to the outer side of the elbow where the strong extensor muscles of the fingers and the wrist attach to the prominent outer bone or epicondyle or the lower point of the humerus. This is known as the common extensor origin.

These powerful muscles insert, without a tendon, directly into the bone and regular prolonged activity of these muscles typical in tennis can give rise to chronic injury and pain.

Cause

It occurs because the body's normal strengthening process has been overloaded. Before it can build up the strength in the muscles and the bone attachments, they have been damaged and each further activity of the muscle pulls on the damaged area injuring it even more.

Treatment

This is clearly a vicious circle and in the first instance the treatment is simply rest, an anathema to the sportsperson. Local ultrasound, injection treatment and occasionally surgery is sometimes indicated in the medical care of tennis elbow. Some people find the use of strapping round the upper forearm helps to off-load the area and protect it. Although it inevitably settles with time it may reduce the performance of your elbow for many months or years and is very painful and disabling.

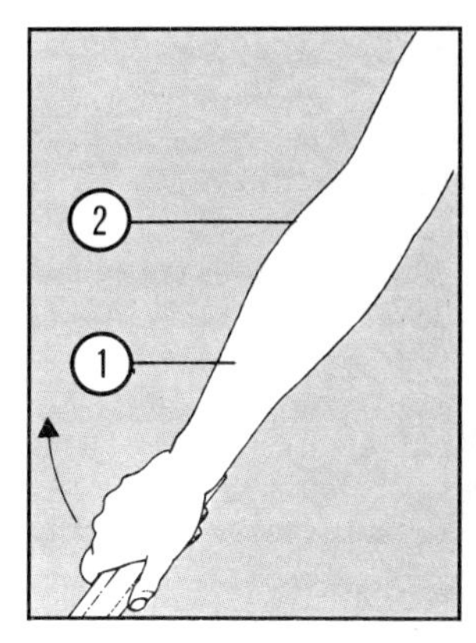

The forearm muscles (1) attach to bone at the elbow (2) and it is at this point that pain from tennis elbow is felt. As it is confined to such a small area, it is suitable for a single local injection which reduces the inflammation.

Prevention

Prevention comes from gradually building up activity rather than going straight back into such racket sports at the beginning of each season without preparation. Take note of any early warning signs of local pain and tenderness and allow a couple of weeks complete rest for these to settle down before building up activities again. Resist the enormous temptation just to swallow a couple of anti-inflammatory tablets and bash on with the sport regardless. Once the injury cycle has started it can be increasingly difficult to break.

Golfer's elbow

This is identical to tennis elbow but occurs on the inner side of the elbow where the strong flexor muscles of the fingers and wrist insert to the inner bony prominence of the elbow. The symptoms are much the same as is the treatment and prevention.

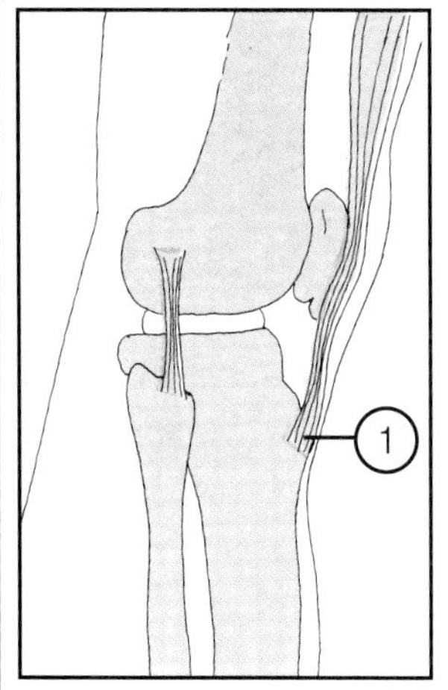

Osgood Schlatter's disease is not in fact a disease but an overuse injury. The bony knob (1) just below the knee joint becomes enlarged and painful to touch. Activities which use a bent knee, such as climbing the stairs, are painful.

Osgood Schlatter's disease

Despite its rather glorious sounding name, this is another form of overuse injury. It occurs in children where the strong tendon coming down from the kneecap attaches to the upper part of the shin.

It is important and worth mentioning because not only is it common but it highlights a particular principle. The point of insertion is an active growing part of a child's skeleton, and is therefore very weak at the site compared with adult bone making injury more likely.

There is not doubt that some individuals are prone to this and in that sense it can't be described as truly avoidable but the same is true of many of these conditions. Nevertheless, it typically occurs in youngsters who are very keen on sport, especially running and football.

Treatment

This is nearly always symptomatic, i.e. strict rest off sport and very occasionally plaster treatment. Surgery has very little part to play. As the child grows and matures it rarely causes further problems.

Prevention

The avoidance of resistive exercises in the lower limb of children is important. Young children should not be pushed too hard in their sport before their skeletons are mature enough to stand the extra activity. Take note of early signs of concern, rest the limb early and completely to avoid getting into the vicious circle.

Groin strain

This is another insertion type problem. It commonly affects footballers and is felt as a pain within the groin where the strong muscles which pull the leg inwards (adductors) attach on to the lower point of the pelvis.

Treatment and prevention

Its treatment is rest, local ultrasound, perhaps physiotherapy and occasionally injection and the avoidance of this condition is once again to build up activity gradually, use stretching exercises properly and warm up adequately before sports. Complete rest early in the condition prevents it from becoming a recurring problem.

Tenosynovitis

This condition can be a feature of the rheumatological disorders such as rheumatoid arthritis which we will deal with later, but more often it's due to overuse of a tendon which is used repetitively and causing inflammation within the synovial sheath resulting in swelling and pain.

De Quervain's

Tenosynovitis occurs at the wrist, on the back of the thumb side, just above the wrist joint. It can occur after prolonged and unusual activity such as painting or typing. The following day this area is exquisitely tender and any attempt to touch it or move the wrist causes very sharp pain. Occasionally creaking (crepitus) can be felt where the tendon is trying to move through the inflamed and tightened sheath. The treatment is complete rest aided by ultrasound and ice and occasionally steriod injections by the doctor.

Achilles' tendinitis

A similar condition which affects the achilles' tendon at the heel. It occurs in runners and can also be caused by ill fitting footwear with a high heel cuff rubbing on the achilles' tendon for prolonged periods. The symptoms are the same, the pain often so sharp it feels like a blister.

Treatment

Rest and supportive measures as outlined above with a slow return to activity and avoidance of the precipitating activity until a gradual build up has been made.

Painful arc

The shoulder is also a site of such overuse injury. The rotator cuff of muscles (see page 21) can become inflamed as can the synovial tissue around the tendon. Once again

Some people are more prone to overuse injuries than others but nevertheless many of them are truly avoidable. The main message is worth repeating:

- *Be aware of what you can reasonably expect of your body.*
- *If you are going to undertake unusual activity or return to a winter or summer sport after prolonged rest do a bit of preparation in advance.*
- *Limber up as described in the warm up section of fitness.*
- *Start gradually.*
- *Don't plan too vigorous or prolonged an activity.*
- *Stop regularly to check.*

Many of these conditions present later in life and the message is even more important in your thirties and forties than in your teens and twenties. Don't be afraid to stop and give the area time to settle down and rest.

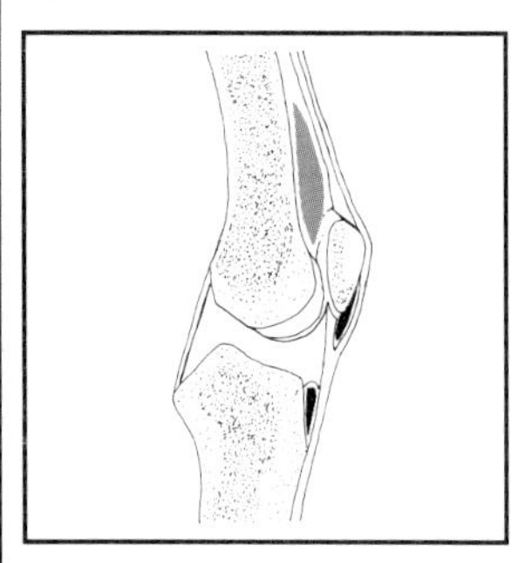

***Bursae** are fluid-filled sacs. They are situated at points in the body where there would normally be friction, for example, over bony points near the skin to prevent the skin rubbing on the underlying bone. There is a bursa under the point of your elbow known as the olecranon bursa, are bursae around the knee, in front of the kneecap (the pre-patellar bursa) and one on the outer side of the hip over the trochanter known as the trochanteric bursa.*

These give perfectly good trouble-free service unless they are overused or abused in which case they become inflamed, swell up and give rise to what is known as bursitis.

the cause is often vigorous and unusual activity such as painting a ceiling or an early season vigorous game of tennis. It is called a painful arc because pain is experienced when the arm is moved away from the body in an arc of 60°-120°. The pain is very severe and there is local tenderness just as the other conditions. It responds in the same way to complete rest and local physiotherapy if necessary.

Bursitis

In olecranon bursitis (elbow), in pre-patellar bursitis or housemaid's knee, and trochanteric bursitis (hip), there is a good predisposing cause for the condition, such as prolonged and unusual kneeling, leaning on the point of the elbow for prolonged periods of time or resting it on a window ledge in a car.

Backache

Much chronic backache (i.e. prolonged pain) is not completely avoidable, nor is the common prolapsed intervertebral disc with which it is often associated. There are certainly many things that you can do to reduce the risk of this disorder and similarly if you do suffer from this condition there are many ways that you can help yourself recover and make your life easier.

Chronic backache is one of the major scourges of working men and women and the cause of the highest number of lost days a year. Not only does it cause huge suffering to individuals but also has major financial implications for the whole country. Yet despite the enormous amount of research into the problems of the back, we are still a long way from understanding many of the actual sites and causes of pain and a long way from certain cures.

In order to come to terms with their problem, it is essential that people with chronic back discomfort have a deep understanding of the problem. The educational approach in the form of back schools is the current trend in the attempt to help people with this difficult problem and, more important, help them help themselves. We now look at some of the recognized pathology or identifiable problems that occur within the back, particularly slipped disc.

Sciatica

The commonest site for a slipped disc is between the fifth lumbar vertebra and the upper part of the sacrum. At this level the trapped nerve is one of the main branches of the sciatic nerve which runs down the back of the leg, around the side of the calf and on to the top of the foot. Pressure on this nerve gives rise to the pain called sciatica. There is of course nothing wrong with the leg but the body doesn't know that. It is getting signals from the sciatic nerve and assumes that is where the pain is coming from so the pain is felt in the leg rather than the site of the injury in the lower back.

Causes

The disc usually 'slips' as a sudden event and often when you are lifting, carrying or twisting. Unfortunately it as often occurs with a very simple manoeuvre such as bending down to tie your shoelaces. The pain in the back and leg is usually immediate and very severe. It causes the lumbar muscles to go into spasm which adds to the problem.

Occasionally the pressure on the nerve is so severe that it damages its function causing weakness and sensory disturbance in the leg giving rise to tingling or even numbness. Very rarely it is so severe and the damage so great that surgery has to be considered to relieve the nerve pressure but this is by far the exception rather than the rule.

Treatment

In most cases the condition can be treated with strict bed rest, strong painkillers and relaxants such as valium. After a period of two to three weeks of this treatment the pain will settle, the swelling around the nerve and the prolapsed material will subside and the material will gradually reabsorb. Over a period of some weeks, often with the benefit of physiotherapy in the form of muscle exercises and stretching, the symptoms will slowly settle and life can resume as normal.

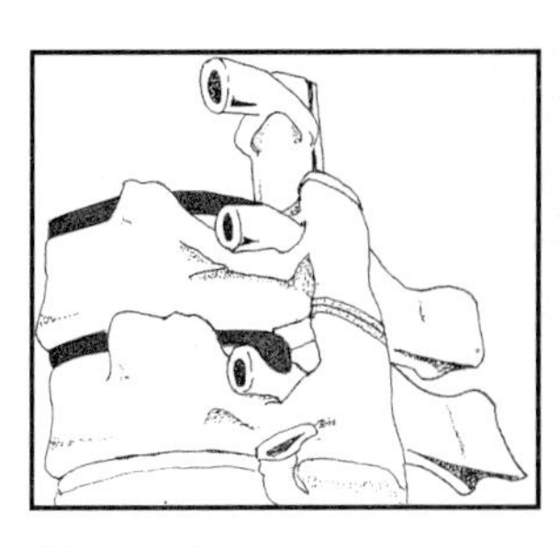

Slipped disc

The intervertebral discs in the healthy adult can be as much as a centimetre deep and are not discs of tissue so much as jelly filled bags. With age the jelly thickens, becomes more degenerate and thicker, the surrounding capsule becomes somewhat stretched and weaker. A 'slipped disc' occurs when one of these discs ruptures and the central material extrudes. The actual amount of material extruding is as little as 1cc or quarter of a teaspoon and yet its position is critical. Due to the arrangements of the strong ligaments around the disc it tends to push out at the back and side of the disc at exactly the point where the spinal nerves exit from the spinal canals. The nerve is therefore pressed, and because it's running through a bony tunnel between the vertebrae above and below, it is unable to move out of the way. This gives rise not only to local pain but also pain in the region of the nerve distribution itself.

Avoiding a prolapsed disc
Even with the best will in the world some fit, healthy people taking great care of themselves get slipped discs but there are one or two cardinal rules. The first is to take care lifting and carrying as outlined in the acute muscle strain section (see page 51.) Awkward lifting, bending the back rather than the legs, and trying to lift something too heavy for you, will all increase the risk of a slipped disc. It is always better to err on the side of caution and stay well within your bounds when you lift.

Late effects of slipped disc

Unfortunately once the disc has been prolapsed in this way the disc height is reduced, its shock absorbency effect is lost and the joints of the back, the intervertebral joints on either side of the backbone, get increased stress and wear out. This commonly leads to osteoarthritis which causes pain in its own right but also the joints become larger and in their own turn press on the nerve. This gives rise to symptoms not dissimilar to the original slipped disc but often with more backache rather than leg pain. This unfortunately does not usually settle down with quite the same speed as the slipped disc in the acute phase and often causes chronic low back discomfort. Treatment for this is often painkillers, anti-inflammatories and local physiotherapy. Once again surgical treatment has a limited part to play.

Abdominal muscles

There is another aspect of general body fitness, which takes us back to the importance of being generally fit and in particular of normal weight. Good muscular strength and posture in the muscles of the abdomen are just as important as the condition of the muscles of the back.

It is easy to see why the muscles of the back are important in prevention of back strain but the importance of the abdominal muscles (tummy muscles) needs a little more explanation. Your abdomen, below your diaphragm and above your pelvis, is surrounded only by the muscles of the abdominal wall. This acts as a muscular bag. You can increase the pressure within it enormously by contracting the muscles against the resistance of holding your breath. (This happens automatically when you cough building up the pressure and releasing it suddenly to expel whatever it is you have inhaled.) In medical terms it is called doing a Valsalva manoeuvre. You also use it subconsciously in bowel evacuation and childbirth.

It is also used as a mechanism for supporting the back in the form of a pneumatic splint. By blowing up your abdomen, as it were, at the front you create a huge stiffness in your trunk and this supports your back muscles and off-loads your discs. This is the basis of the large belt that weight-lifters strap round their abdomens and is why you hold your breath when you try and lift anything heavy. If you allow yourself to get very overweight and your abdominal muscles weaken it is much more difficult to bring this important anatomical support into play and consequently your back is less supported and more likely to be injured.

Chronic backache (lumbago)

Chronic backache, i.e. low back pain of long duration, is sometimes called lumbago and it may arise as a result of an old prolapsed intervertebral disc and sciatica as described above. It may occur as the result of an acute back sprain as described on page 51, or it may come without warning and develop insidiously over a period of time. It might be a feature of early degenerative change (osteoarthritis) and this condition will be dealt with in detail later, but quite often clinical examination by the doctor and X-rays fail to show any obvious abnormality and it's impossible to pin-point an anatomical cause for the problem. It is often described as a chronic ligament sprain and it may be related to the type of overuse injuries already described, point of insertion of muscles and tendons never being allowed to fully recover.

Treatment

The treatment for this condition tends to be somewhat empirical. Active exercises and physiotherapy to mobilize the spine is valuable in some individuals, complete rest in the form of bed rest, a corset or plaster jackets are useful in others. Some form of pain-killer or anti-inflammatory drug is nearly always valuable as an adjunct.

Time alone will often settle the problem but it may become a problem for life and the individual will have to come to terms with this while medical science seeks an answer.

Coping with chronic back pain

Take note of all the advice about care of your back in terms of lifting and carrying and adjust your day-to-day life if possible to avoid these activities or modify them.

Make sure that you aren't overweight. There is no doubt that this contributes to the pain of chronic backache. Unfortunately, back pain often reduces your ability to exercise, and this in turn makes it difficult to keep your weight down and so the vicious cycle continues. However, swimming is a good aerobic and supportive form of exercise and is often very valuable if you have access to this facility. This not only may help with weight reduction but also keeps the muscles fit in terms of strength and endurance. There is no doubt that weaker backs hurt more than stronger backs. The good news in this condition is that it tends to wax and wane and unless you get into a deep vicious circle of increasing weight gain and lack of fitness, you can often tide yourself over until the next natural remission in symptoms during which time you can improve on general fitness. However, it is most important to remember to take great care to avoid any predisposing activity.

Strengthening exercises

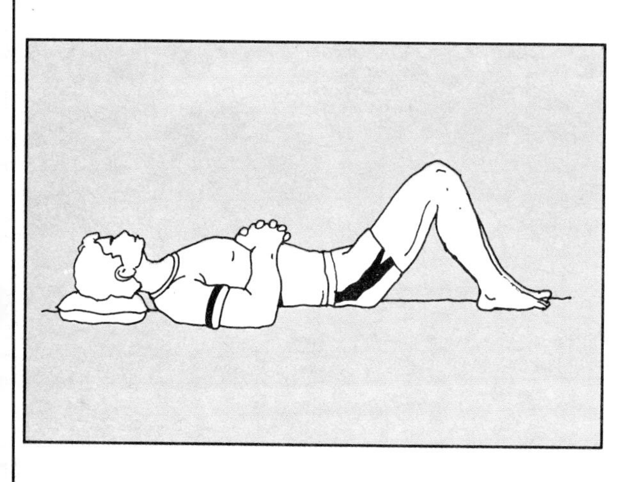

If you're very unfit, overweight or suffering from acute back pain, consult your medical practitioner before embarking on any exercise programme. Even if you're not, don't overdo new things to start with. You can expect to feel some stretching in your muscles and joints, but stop if you feel anything more than mild discomfort: the idea is to feel stretch, not pain.
The following routine is on two levels of difficulty. Only go on to the second when you feel comfortable with the first. Do them every day if you can to help prevent or relieve chronic pain; you'll still find them useful two or three times a week. Keep movements smooth and controlled: don't jerk.

Level 1
1. Resting position (above)
Lie flat, head on a small cushion, knees bent, hands on abdomen. Breathe gently and deeply; feel your hands move as you do. Starting at toes and working up to head and face, check muscles for tension and let it go. Don't start exercises until you're relaxed. Continue breathing deeply and regularly throughout: try not to hold your breath.

2. Knee to chest (right)
Draw knee slowly towards chest as far as possible without pain. Hold for a slow count of five; return to resting position. Repeat four times with each leg, then with both at same time. Use muscles in legs to move them, not arms, though you should feel slight stretch in arms. (Good for stretching whole of lower back.)

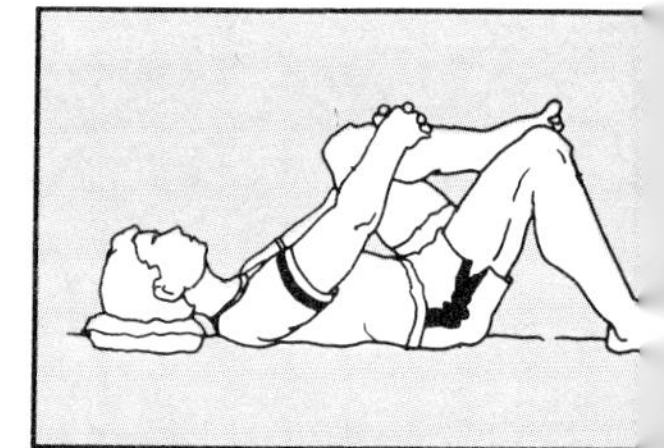

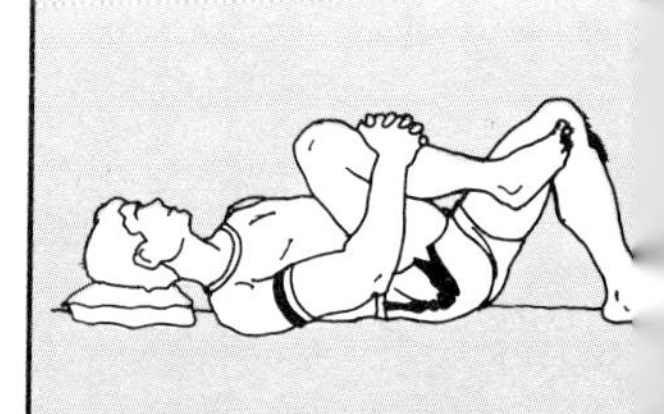

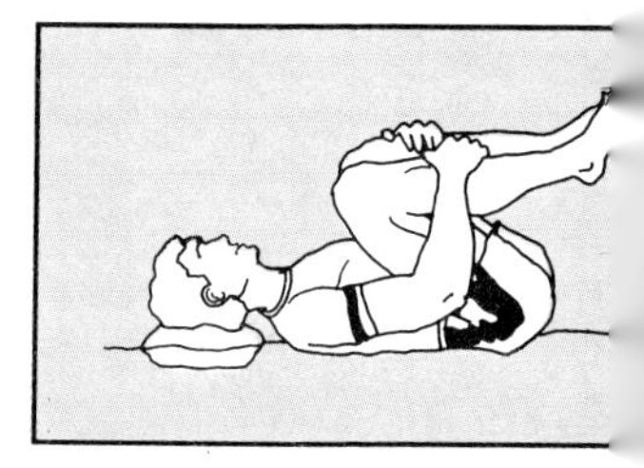

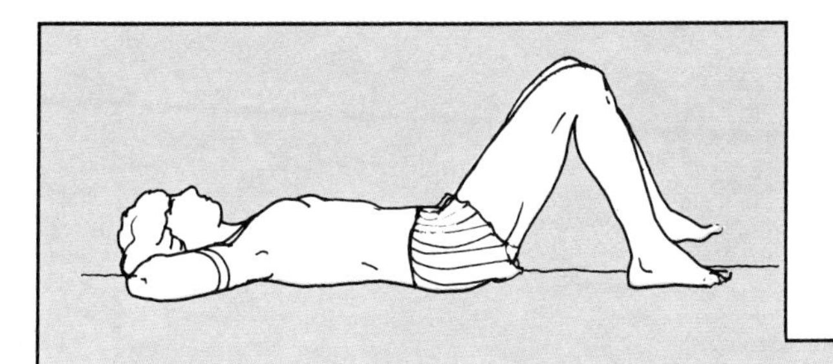

3. Pelvic tilt (1)
(above and right)
In resting position, clench buttocks and tilt pelvis up. Feel spine flatten against floor, but don't try to help it by using abdominal muscles or legs. Hold for a slow count of five; relax. Repeat, gradually working up to 10 repetitions.

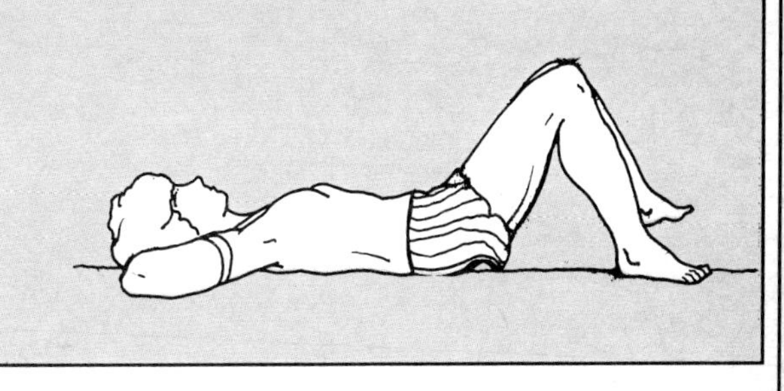

4. Pelvic tilt (2)
(right and below)
Starting in resting position, clench buttocks as if for pelvic tilt (1), but this time use abdominal muscles too so that hips lift off floor. Hold for a slow count of five; relax. Repeat up to 10 times.

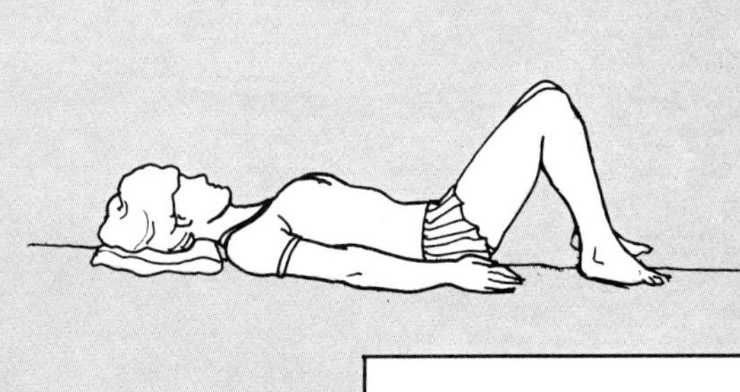

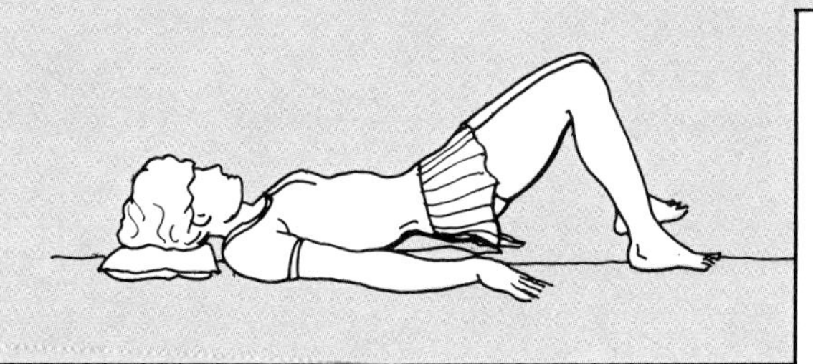

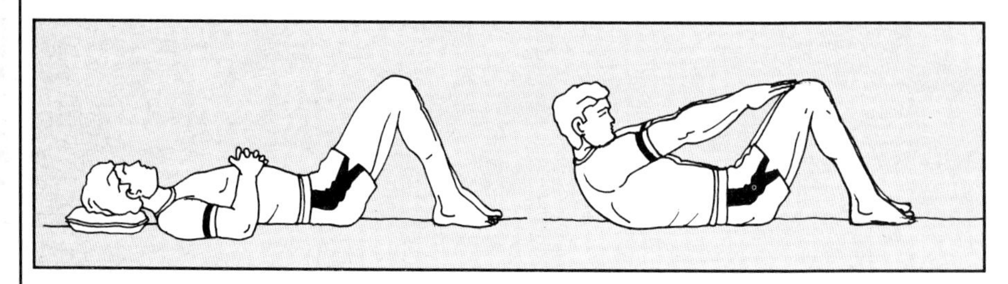

5. Sit-ups (above)
From resting position, slowly raise head, neck and upper body as you reach for your knees. Keep middle and bottom of back on floor. Hold with hands gently on knees for a slow count of five; relax. Repeat up to 10 times.

6. Hamstring stretch (below)
From resting position, stretch right leg flat along floor. Raise it slowly until you feel pain or tightness in back of thigh; keep it straight. Hold for a slow count of five; lower slowly. Repeat up to 10 times with each leg, keeping back flat on floor and arms behind head.

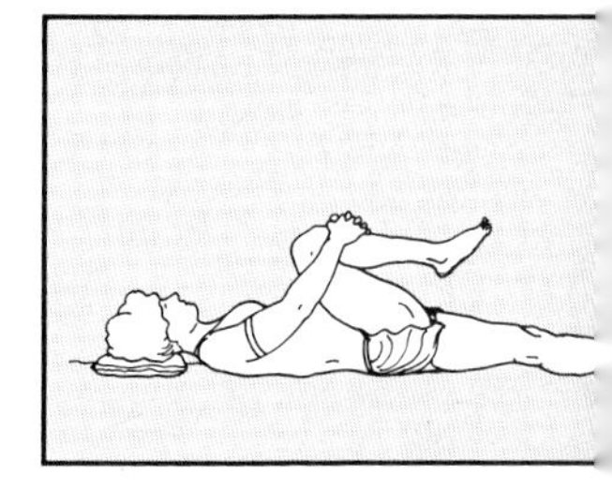

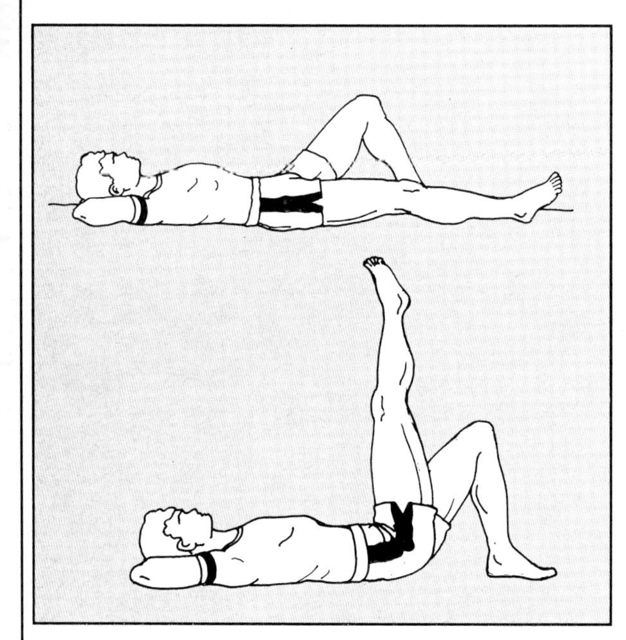

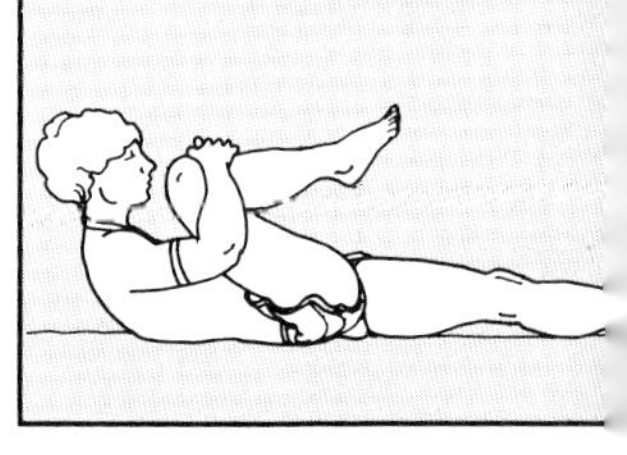

7. Knee to nose (above)
From resting position, bring one knee slowly to chest, clasp it with both hands. Extend other leg so it's flat on floor. Keep lower back on floor; slowly raise head, neck and upper shoulders until your nose gets as near to your knee as it comfortably can. Hold for a slow count of five; slowly relax. Repeat up to 10 times with each leg.

8. Hamstring and achilles' stretch (right top)
Sit with one knee bent. Keep other leg flat on floor with sole of foot against a wall. Bend forward slowly until you feel stretch at back of straight leg. Hold for a slow count of five; relax. Repeat up to 10 times with each leg.

9. Standing calf and achilles' tendon stretch (right below)
Stand with front half of feet across a thick book 30-60 cms (1'-2') from a wall. Place palms against wall. Keeping legs straight, slowly lean forwards to wall until you feel stretch in calves and achilles' tendons at back of heels; hold for a slow count of five. Repeat up to 15 times.

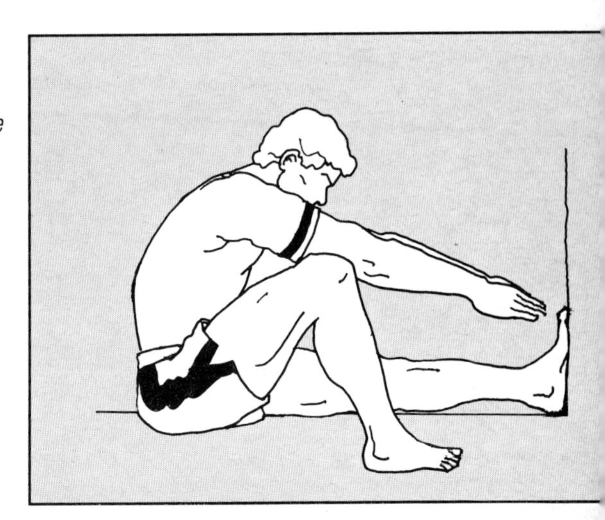

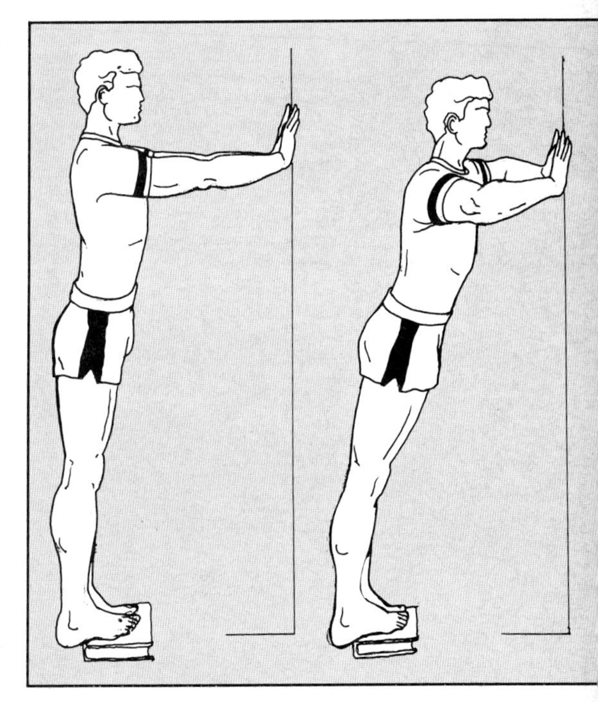

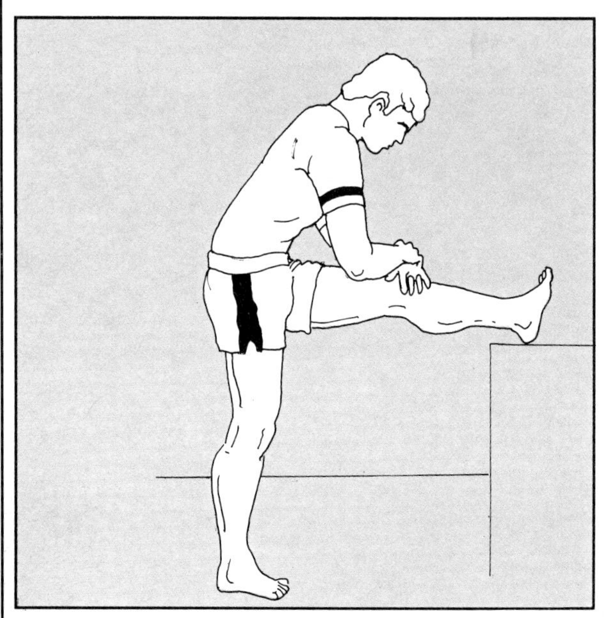

2. Hip roll (below)
Lie flat on back, arms out at sides. Bend knees so feet come close to buttocks. Keeping knees together and close to chest, slowly roll them towards floor. Come back slowly to starting position; repeat to opposite side. Repeat entire exercise up to eight times.

Level 2

1. Standing hamstring stretch (above)
From a standing position, place heel on low chair. Keep both legs straight; slowly lean forward until you feel stretch in hamstrings. Repeat up to 10 times for each leg.

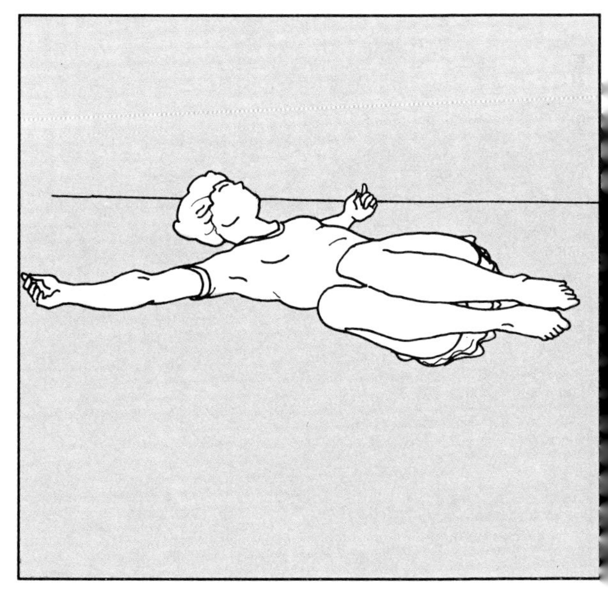

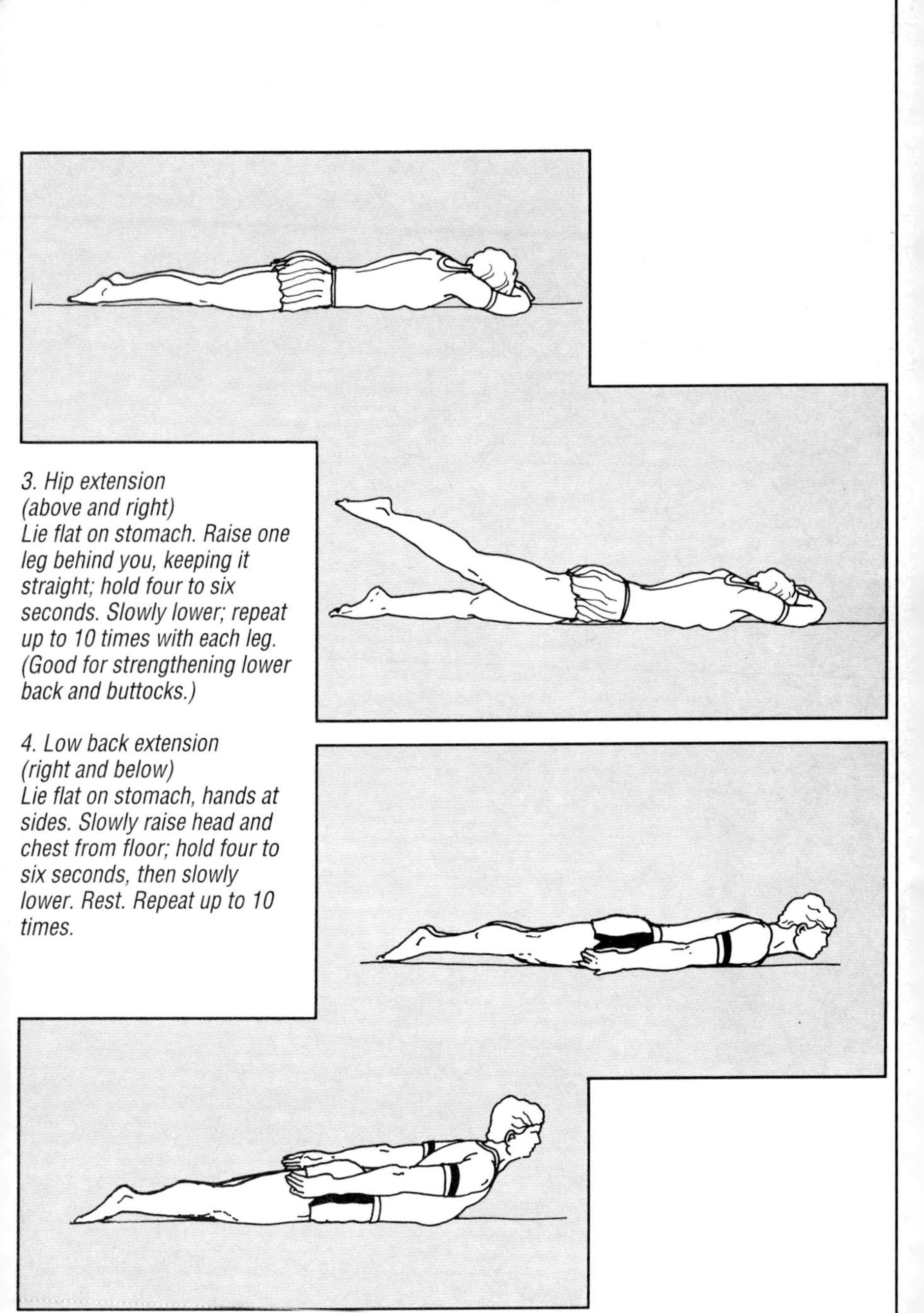

3. Hip extension
(above and right)
Lie flat on stomach. Raise one leg behind you, keeping it straight; hold four to six seconds. Slowly lower; repeat up to 10 times with each leg. (Good for strengthening lower back and buttocks.)

4. Low back extension
(right and below)
Lie flat on stomach, hands at sides. Slowly raise head and chest from floor; hold four to six seconds, then slowly lower. Rest. Repeat up to 10 times.

Preventing and alleviating osteoporosis

As yet there is no known cure for this condition, i.e. we know of no way of increasing bone bulk once it is lost. It is therefore critical, particularly in women, that they build up as much bone as they can in their early adult life.

Osteoporosis

Osteoporosis is sometimes called the adult brittle bone disease. The term is not entirely applicable as it doesn't fully describe what is happening in osteoporosis. In medical terminology brittle bone disease is used for the much rarer and more serious fragile bones in children which is a congenital disorder. Osteoporosis on the other hand is extremely common and it particularly affects women. It has been receiving increasing attention in the popular press and a certain amount of confusion exists. However, although it is very common, the important message is that it may well be highly preventable but you have to take action young.

What is osteoporosis?

Osteoporosis is a natural condition of an ageing skeleton in which the bone becomes weaker because there is effectively less of it. The size of your bones doesn't decrease, but the quantity of bone material within each bone itself is less. A dry bone from a young person would weigh more than a dry bone from an older person even if they were exactly the same size.

The amount of bone you have is at a peak when you are between twenty and thirty years old, i.e. you increase your bone mass for some years after you stop growing and this is readily observed in the maturing individual after growth stops in the late teens. From then on there is a steady decline in the amount of bone in your body. However, men start off with more bone in their bodies than women, so this decline is not noticeable as early as it is in women.

Another particular problem is that women have a sudden increased loss of bone at the time of the menopause or change of life and this is due to hormonal factors. It can be clearly seen therefore that if in a woman bone mass wasn't very great and she had an early menopause, she may run out of bone early in her old age and the features of osteoporosis may well present.

If the bones become weaker they are more likely to break. This may be caused by an injury such as a fall onto the outstretched hand or may occur spontaneously which typically occurs in the spine.

Osteoporosis and injury

Two of the commonest fractures that present to the hospital resulting from falls both occur in women in their later years. In both cases osteoporosis is implicated. That is not to say that if you have had one of these fractures you necessarily have osteoporosis but it is commonly the cause.

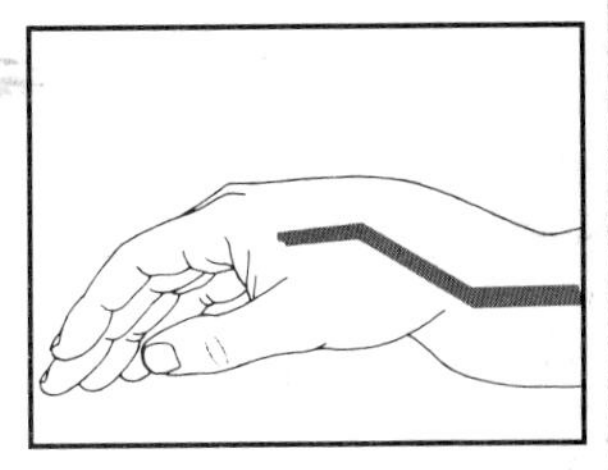

Colles' fracture

This is caused by a fall onto an outstretched arm. The bone that fractures is actually the end of the radius in the forearm. It is much commoner in women in late middle age.

The bone adopts the typical dinner fork deformity and is treated by manipulation under anaesthetic (setting the fracture) and six weeks in a plaster cast. The wrist is rather stiff after this but responds to physiotherapy given time. Good function nearly always follows, although a bony prominence or bump may persist.

Fracture of neck of femur

This occurs in much older women. The femur is the thigh bone and the fracture occurs just at the top below the hip joint. In many individuals osteoporosis is a factor although this injury occurs typically in elderly and sometimes confused individuals who may have sustained a fracture because they are more likely to fall than other people. This whole subject is still an area of great debate but nevertheless osteoporosis has probably a significant part to play.

The elderly woman typically falls without significant predisposing cause and is unable to get up because of pain in the groin and hip from the fracture. The treatment is almost always an operation to replace the broken fragment of bone with a metal part or to pin the bones together depending on where the fracture has occurred. The recovery tends to be rather slow but many of these elderly women do return home to continue an independent existence.

Spontaneous fracturing in osteoporosis

As well as the traumatic fracturing as described above a more insidious problem that occurs with osteoporosis is spontaneous squashing down of the vertebral bodies in the spine. This usually occurs in the cervical and lumbar spinal regions and because the bone collapses in the body of the vertebrae, i.e. at the front of the bone, the bone tends to angulate. This gives rise to the typical round spined appearance of the old lady or what used to be called rather

Summary
Osteoporosis is at the moment incurable once it presents and there is little we can currently do to increase bone mass. However, a good exercise regime and diet during the first half of your life with calcium supplements in women at risk will probably prevent much of this problem and the related suffering until medical science finds a way of reversing this trend of bone loss with advancing age.

unfairly dowager's hump. These spontaneous fractures may occur at several levels within the spine and pass almost unnoticed except that gradually the patient notices that she's lost height and changed shape. In some instances a specific episode of crush can be remembered and of course they may also occur as a result of a fall. There is almost never an indication for specific treatment of these other than pain relief but sometimes a corset will help support the painful area. Surgery is quite inappropriate as the bones are thin and soft and respond badly to any operative technique.

Over the course of a period of some weeks the pain gradually resolves and the patient will return to the previous level of activity albeit with a slightly shorter and more curved spine. In most cases, this is more of a nuisance than a major disability. There is no doubt that there are increasing numbers of people reaching old age and increasing numbers of people who are very severely affected and disabled by this insidious condition. This is why it has taken on prominence in the public press.

Other risk factors

It would appear that there are other factors which affect bone loss as well as the commoner ones outlined above. This information has been gathered by looking at large numbers of people suffering from the condition and certain factors emerge. There seems to be a familial element to it. If your mother or aunts have had the condition you are probably more at risk.

Smoking once again rears its ugly head and smokers appear to get osteoporosis more commonly than non-smokers. The exact reason for this is not clear and it's possible that it's got something to do with diet and exercise. Being excessively thin also predisposes towards osteoporosis.

Osteoporosis and osteoarthritis

These two conditions offer major problems that will affect your active body with advancing age. The majority of hospital admissions to orthopedic units are as a result of a

Bone building

• Exercise

It would appear that exercise is the key. There is little doubt now that by taking exercise in your youth, i.e. up to the age of mid-thirties, the body will respond by making more bone. This follows all the principles about the body's response to use. In your youth it has the ability to build up its structure in response to your demands on it. There has been some debate about the type of exercise that is best, i.e. whether strong peak activity is better than prolonged activity, and as yet this is somewhat unsettled but there is some evidence to support peak effort as being more important. However, the main message is take exercise, use your bones and build them up early in life.

• Diet

Healthy bones need to be supported by a healthy diet but unfortunately there is no evidence that large quantities of calcium, for example, will build up your bones once you have established osteoporosis. However, it is important to have adequate calcium in your diet when you are young, especially if you are a woman, so that you can make the most of your exercise programmes and build up good bone. A normal balanced diet still provides enough calcium as long as it includes some dairy products. This is in some conflict with advice from doctors to reduce the level of dairy products because of the risks of cardiovascular disease but can be got round by using skimmed milk or other reduced fat products which have high calcium levels. The only indications in most people for calcium supplements is in pregnancy and lactation or if you have a specific problem or illness which reduces your ability to absorb it.

• Sex hormones

The effect of the menopause, and thus loss of certain sex hormones from the circulation, on bone mass is discussed on page 66 and clearly one way of preventing that bone loss and thus osteoporosis symptoms later on is to give individuals hormone supplements. In some cases this is done. There are some problems associated with the use of hormone supplements but nevertheless they would appear to be valuable in certain circumstances. The general feeling in the medical profession at the moment is that in women who are at a high risk (see below) and/or have developed early features of bone thinning and who have an early menopause, then the risks of hormone replacement are justifiable. Bone loss can be reduced but at the moment widespread use of hormones in post menopausal women is not considered to be the answer to the problem of osteoporosis.

manifestation of one of the two. One fascinating fact is that the two conditions are almost exclusive of one another, i.e. people with osteoporosis tend not to get osteoarthritis and this is particularly so of the hip. People with fractured neck of femur very rarely have or will develop osteoarthritis of the hip but the exact reason for this remains obscure.

Unavoidable conditions

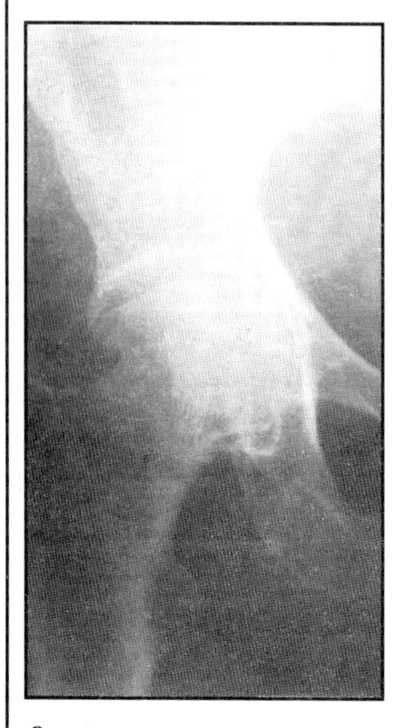

Causes

In osteoarthritis, the shiny surface (the articular cartilage) of your joints begins to wear out and break down. The exact reason for this is quite unknown but unfortunately the body is not able to repair damaged articular cartilage. As it wears down fragments of it become loose in the joint and irritate the lining (the synovium) of that joint which responds by producing fluid. This causes an effusion (water on the joint).

The joint makes attempts to repair and throws out small bony buttresses around the joint known as osteophytes (see above). These, however, are unsuccessful in halting the condition and eventually all the shiny surface wears off

Osteoarthritis

Osteoarthritis is not an avoidable condition. It is an age accelerated disorder which means that as time passes on nearly everyone over 55 will have some degree of osteoarthritic change. Nevertheless, the relationship between having the condition in the joints and getting symptoms from it, i.e. suffering from it, is not clear cut. There are many things one can do to alleviate the suffering from it and as we are all liable to get the condition, we need to know what it is.

Osteoarthritis is the commonest form of arthritis and is often known as old age or wear and tear, or degenerative arthritis. It is different from the inflammatory or reactive arthritides, the most common and typical example of which is rheumatoid arthritis which will be dealt with later. Although it is very common in the elderly, it is not simply a feature of getting old as some people can reach the grand old age of 100 without having any signs of it whatsoever. It would appear that there is a strong genetic component to it and some families have individuals affected early, especially on the female side. What is also clear is that it can occur as a result of injury or overuse of individual joints. It tends to affect only certain joints (which is different to the inflammatory arthritis which can affect any joint). Osteoarthritis is common in the back, the neck, the hips and knees, the big toe and the little joints at the ends of your fingers and, especially in women, the base of the thumb. The arthritis doesn't necessarily spread to all these areas in any individual and just because you develop the features of it in one joint early in your middle years doesn't necessarily imply it will spread anywhere else.

Treatment

Early in the condition simple anti-inflammatory tablets such as Brufen can be taken which reduces the joint's inflammatory reaction. It does not, of course, repair the shiny surface or reduce the damage but does relieve the pain and often improves the range of movement by reduced the swelling.

Although the joint damage is progressive, the symptoms may be cyclical for no obvious reason, i.e. you may have a bad spell with it for some months, it responds to some anti-inflammatories and then recurs the following year.

The other form of treatment which is valuable is physiotherapy to build muscle strength and reduce swelling. In many cases these supportive measures do not give long-term benefit and occasionally surgery is needed.

Surgical treatment

One of the commonest operations in the practice of orthopedic surgery is total hip replacement for osteoarthritis. This is a wonderful and effective pain-relieving operation which allows continued range of movement and is one of the great success stories of recent years in Western medicine. Although total hips are the commonest replacements, knee replacements are becoming increasingly successful and other joints too such as shoulder and elbow are also being done but in much smaller numbers. However, sometimes such large and dramatic surgery is not necessary in smaller joints such as the fingers. Simple fusion of the joint gets rid of the pain but of course gives rise to a permanent stiffness. Excision of part of the joint, i.e. taking away one side of it, is an effective manoeuvre in some cases and this is often done in the big toe.

Alleviation in osteoarthritis

Although osteoarthritis is not avoidable, maintaining good shape, normal weight and physical fitness will often significantly benefit you. There is no evidence that being obese causes osteoarthritis even though the extra weight might be expected to cause more damage to the joints. What is known, however, from various well described studies, is that being overweight causes osteoarthritis to hurt more and this is a very real way that you can reduce the pain, for example, in an osteoarthritic knee.

Similarly it has been well described that building up the muscles around the leg will relieve the pain of osteoarthritis of the knee. Exactly why this is so is not quite clear but in the absence of any other remedy of an imme-

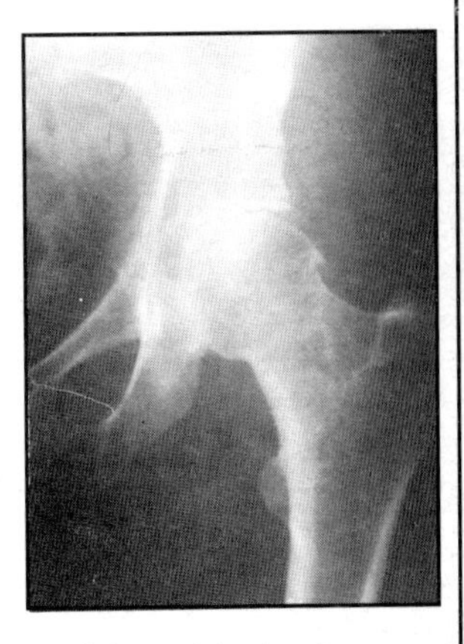

the joint and the two bone ends start rubbing together one on the other. All this gives rise to pain, swelling and stiffness. The picture of the X-ray demonstrates the normal joint with healthy rounded bone ends with a generous space between them which of course is filled with a shiny surface (above). The lower X-ray demonstrates the pattern in osteoarthritis.

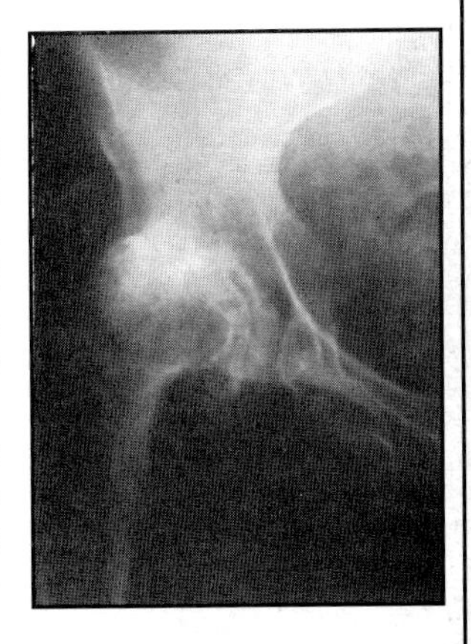

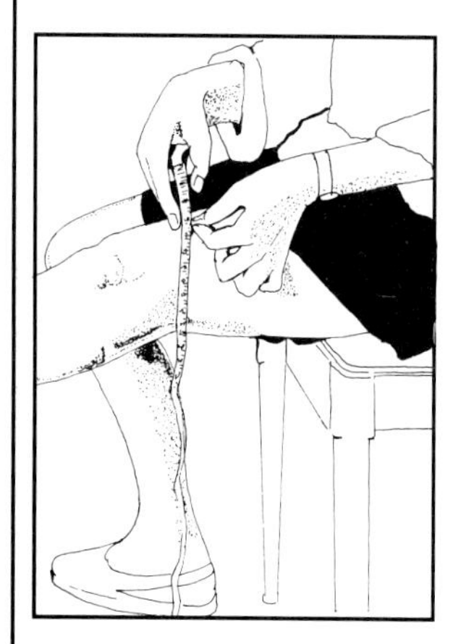

Alleviating osteoarthritis
You can measure the thigh bulk with a tape measure to assess your progress taking care of course to measure it at the same height, about 10 cm above the kneecap with the knee straight. If you set clear goals of muscle build-up, over the months you can certainly produce a better muscle which is almost inevitably associated with reduction in pain. Once again it needs stressing that the arthritis won't go away - the joint damage has been done and is continuing - but the pain will be alleviated to some extent.

diate nature it is certainly worth persisting with a home exercise regime designed to build up the quadriceps and hamstrings.

Osteoarthritis of the spine

This is such a big area that it deserves mention in its own right. It is common in the low back where it is known as lumbar spondylosis and as I have already said may arise from an old slipped disc or it may arise on its own without evidence of old disc disease.

In the cervical spine it is known as cervical spondylosis and is one of the most common sites of arthritis in the body. The sacrum and coccyx are never significantly affected and the thoracic spine very rarely so.

Cervical spondylosis

Arthritis occurs in the small joints between the cervical vertebrae. It develops gradually, without any initial predisposing and/or obvious cause. However, it may occur secondary to a slipped disc in the neck, but this is less common than it is in the low lumbar region.

Development

The arthritis builds up in the small joints giving rise to stiffness and local pain in the neck. This often spreads down over the top of the shoulder. People mistakenly think they have arthritis in the shoulder but actually it's pain referred down from the neck. In fact, osteoarthritis of the shoulder is extremely uncommon.

As the joints become worn down they enlarge as in the lumbar spine by the growth of osteophytes. These encroach on the holes from which the spinal nerves are emerging. In the case of the neck these nerves are going down the arm and so pressure on them gives rise to pain in the arm and the fingers. This may be accompanied by tingling and occasionally true numbness and weakness if the nerves are seriously involved.

Sometimes the pain or sensory disturbance in the arm occurs without any obvious neck symptoms at all but an X-ray of the cervical spine will usually find the cause of the problem.

Once again the arthritis, though present and persisting, will not cause continuous symptoms and it is quite typical in the neck that the symptoms wax and wane over the years. Nevertheless, the pain when it does occur is often disabling, and needs specific treatment.

Treatment

This is as for any arthritis, i.e. anti-inflammatory drugs and physiotherapy in the form of local treatment such as heat and exercises. Often supportive treatment with a collar is useful. Just as in chronic low back pain the treatment is somewhat empirical: for example, if exercising helps it one should persist with that; if keeping it still helps reduce the pain, a collar will be the line to adopt. This often appears extremely confusing to an individual patient presenting to the doctor who is told on one visit to move his neck with exercise and on the next one to keep it completely still in a collar. Nevertheless, it is impossible to predict in any individual person who will benefit and therefore it is a matter to some extent of trial and error.

Very rarely surgery is needed to release the nerves or to fuse the spine so that the two vertebral bodies no longer move one on the other. However, this is only necessary in a tiny percentage of cases.

Alleviation of cervical spondylosis

Nearly everyone will have some osteoarthritis in their neck by the time they are forty or fifty and many of us will already have started suffering the occasional symptom in the form of a bit of stiffness or pain by then.

First of all avoid unnecessary injury or strain to your neck. Don't forget the muscles attached to your shoulder girdle and thus your arm are attached to the bones of your neck. Awkward lifting or prolonged carrying can sometimes lead to a strain and give rise to local stiffness. If you have begun to get early symptoms think twice about the wisdom of continuing activities such as contact sports and rugby football in particular which you know will strain the neck. If you are going to continue to play, make sure that you undertake regular flexibility and strengthening exercises to provide extra support.

Posture
Look after your neck posture. An awful lot of people start complaining about neck symptoms after prolonged, reading, typing or work at a desk in which the work height is slightly inappropriate and they have had to adopt a permanent and awkward neck position. Take account of this at home and at work and spend some time adjusting things for your full comfort. These preventative measures are much better than struggling on and then suffering later. Don't be afraid to approach your employer if necessary to provide better equipment if this is going to make a significant difference. He or she would probably rather invest in getting your work environment right than having you off sick for a lengthy period of time.

Exercises

If you do suffer from occasional pain and stiffness in the neck get into the habit of a regular exercise routine to maintain its mobility. This involves stretching type exercises, looking over one shoulder and twisting your head round to look over the other shoulder and tipping your head backwards and forwards. It is no longer recommended that you do a full head roll with your neck fully bent back. Combine these with shoulder shrugging exercises to maintain the posture of your arm because the shoulder girdle and your arms are suspended from your neck with muscle and many neck problems are associated with poor upper shoulder posture.

It is often very difficult to strictly adhere to this sort of exercise programme but if it's going to prevent problems in the future it's worthwhile. A good analogy is to consider the amount of time you spend cleaning your teeth morning and evening to prevent future dental problems. Although not ideal there is an ultimate and final solution for a painful tooth but not always a final and ultimate solution to your painful back and neck.

In most cases the good news with the neck as with the back is that it tends to be cyclical in nature. Although the arthritis doesn't go out of the joints much of the pain will settle for long periods of time before coming back again. While you have good remission of symptoms don't forget your exercises. Maintain your health and fitness as outlined previously and it may well reduce the risk of further trouble. It will certainly help to alleviate it if you get some.

Accidents and injuries

Even if you are a fit, active person and take great care of your body, with the best will in the world disasters do occasionally befall you. These can be grouped into two sections. First true accidents and injuries and secondly unavoidable diseases.

Any of your body's complex structures can be injured. A few basic principles need to be understood to explain how an injury heals and a recovery occurs with particular reference to fractured bones. There are also one or two specific problems such as injuries to the knee which are so common that they are worth dealing with in more detail. Although an accident by definition occurs without warning there are some sensible preventative measures that can be taken. There are two clear principal messages: if you are going to indulge in any activity which risks injury such as driving a car or playing sport, make use of all the available safety equipment; and secondly remember that the fitter and healthier you are before the accident, the quicker you will recover from it and the less likely you are to suffer from long-term problems.

Response to injury

All the components of the musculo-skeletal system have a capacity to heal or repair except for articular cartilage.

Ligaments

Injuries to ligaments (sprains) are very common. The ligament collagen fibres rupture under high strain, blood vessels tear in association and a bruise forms very rapidly. The area swells and is painful.

If protected with appropriate rest and, in some cases, complete immobilization in plaster, the ligament will heal up with scar tissue which is also comprised of collagenous material. In most cases the resulting repair will be nearly as good as the original ligament and no obvious instability will occur. (There are one or two exceptions, one of which is the anterior cruciate ligament of the knee which is so important it will be dealt with separately on page 82.)

There are many partial tears of ligaments or minor sprains in which, because the whole substance is not

• Fracture healing and diet
A broken bone initially needs rest. It also needs a good healthy diet to use for materials to rebuild the broken area. There is, however, no evidence that increased vitamin intake or calcium speeds the process in any way and as long as you have a balanced diet, you will give your body the best chance of healing quickly.

disrupted, treatment with elevation, ice and gentle compression bandage will often result in a satisfactory recovery over a period of a few days or weeks. Occasionally an injury of this nature, especially around the ankle, gives rise to some joint problems possibly due to the lack of joint position sense. In these cases, formal physiotherapy is very valuable in re-educating the muscles and nerves around the joint to restore you to complete function. It is important in dealing with a ligamentous sprain to have a lot of rest early on to allow it to recover well rather than try and get back to your sport or activity too soon. This can give rise to prolonged discomfort and pain and ultimately won't get you back to top performance any quicker.

Tendons

Tendons can rupture and this has been dealt with in the avoidable section with the achilles' tendon but direct injuries can also cause the tendon to rupture if it's on strain at the time. If the tendon doesn't pull apart, as it often can do with the muscle pulling at one end, it will heal up in the same sort of way as a ligament with fibrous tissue. Over a period of about six weeks it will be restored to its full former strength.

Obviously if the tendon itself retracts back it needs to be surgically repaired and immobilized while it heals. Nevertheless, the long term results of tendon repairs are usually good.

Articular cartilage

This material is quite unique in the body in that very little repair occurs. Injuries to joints, therefore, can be the most devastating of all. If the articular cartilage damage is significant, the joint fails giving rise to pain on use and ultimately osteoarthritis.

Muscle

Muscle tissue repairs by a process of fibrosis or scarring rather than by making more muscle itself. This means that if you have had an extensive muscle injury, the volume of muscle you have left will ultimately be less. However, if when the process of healing has occurred you continue with muscle strength exercises, you will be able to enlarge the muscle fibres as described in the fitness section. By making it as strong as possible you may well recover nearly all the function you need for normal activities.

Injury to bones

Despite their enormous strength, bones can be broken. The medical term for a broken bone is a fracture and contrary to popular belief, there is no difference between a fractured and a broken bone. Bone has the capacity to heal completely if properly treated in nearly all circumstances.

Bone healing

The steps are as follows. Immediately the bone breaks, blood is lost from the bone ends and a large bruise occurs around the fracture site. This causes immediate pain, swelling and loss of function of the affected area. If appropriately treated and stabilized, the bruise (hematoma) will become organized by the body as blood vessels and scar tissue cells grow in. This forms what is known as granulation tissue.

However, instead of this going on to give rise to mature fibrous scar tissue, the whole area becomes filled with loosely packed bone, known as callus. On X-ray this appears as white fluffy clouds around the ends of the broken bone and is a sign that the fracture is healing.

As time passes the body remodels and reorganizes this material, gradually the bone is reshaped and all of this callus is removed. The callus therefore acts as a temporary splint while the underlying reparative process continues.

This whole process takes many weeks and months and depends on the bone involved. A fracture of the femur in an adult will take about 12 weeks to be solid enough to walk on and it will be another two years before the bone has completely remodelled. In smaller bones this time is much quicker and in a child of one it's extremely fast indeed, the fracture healing up within a couple of weeks. Within a few months there will be almost no sign that there had ever been a break.

• Helping the bone to heal
You will be given specific instructions about what activities you can and can't undertake from the surgeon treating your fracture and there are two broad principles to observe.

First of all keep the rest of your body as fit and active as you can within the limits of the fracture treatment. Obviously if you have injured a foot you may need to spend some time with it elevated to reduce the swelling but once this has happened keep the rest of your body in as reasonable shape as possible. Don't use an injured limb as an excuse to let it go into decline. If you do, by the time the plaster is removed or the traction taken down you'll find it much slower to get going. Even if you are lying in a hospital bed you can do regular exercises to maintain the muscle strength although clearly aerobic exercises are rather out of the question.

The second principle is that as soon as the doctor lets you take weight through your healing limb or start using it actively, do take this early advice even if initially it is somewhat uncomfortable.

Treatment

This is a huge subject which would readily fill a book several times this size but in outline the following are the principles of current treatment for fractured bones as well as some of the complications and problems.There are seven broad options open to the orthopaedic surgeon in treating your individual fracture.

• Supportive

Here no attempt is made to put the bone ends together but pain relief and simple supportive measures are given. An example of fractures treated in this way would be a collarbone (clavicle) or broken rib. There is no need to attempt specific splinting of these areas as they inevitably go on to give a good long-term result. This doesn't mean that they are any less painful and the treatment in this category is based on trying to relieve the pain and continue function in the associated areas.

• Traction

This is one of the most well-established methods of fracture treatment. It involves pulling on the bone by means of strings attached either to a pin inserted in a bone below the fracture or to a sticky bandage applied to the skin of the limb below the fracture. Putting weights on the string will pull the fracture out to length and immobilize it well enough for it to heal in a good position.

Traction is particularly useful in the long bones of the leg, especially the femur, but also in fractures of the spine, especially the neck. In this latter case traction is applied through a special halo fixed to the skull. The benefits of this approach are that it is minimally invasive. The fracture can heal by normal methods without actively being disturbed but yet allow the patient to move the joints of the affected limb. The disadvantage, of course, is that you are confined to a hospital bed with all its attendant problems.

• Plaster of Paris

This is one of the commonest forms of managing a fracture. It is used where the fracture needs to be held in an accurate position while healing takes place and is particularly useful for fractures of the wrist like the Colles' fracture or fractures of the scaphoid at the base of the thumb. Ankle fractures are also commonly treated by plaster of Paris.

The advantage of this technique is that you can go home and often return to work and it is a relatively simple albeit cumbersome system.

There are one or two risks associated with encasing an injured limb in a cast and one of these is that the skin can get sore underneath where it rubs or the limb can swell and cut off the blood supply. People who have had plasters applied will be given specific instruction about reattending the hospital urgently if there is any pain or tingling in the fingers or toes so that the plaster can be released.

• Open reduction and internal fixation

In this approach the surgeon actually operates on the fractured bone to fix it with plates, screws or pins. This is obviously a more major undertaking than the other treatments but it allows a perfect result in terms of anatomical position and the bones are put back exactly where they belong.

Examples of this technique include fractures involving joints where complete congruity of the joint is important, especially as articular cartilage has no powers of recovery. It is also used where a perfect repositioning of the bones is essential for a good functional result, such as in the bones of the forearm. If these heal only 15° out of alignment it will reduce the ability of the forearm to move properly.

Another advantage of the technique is that it simply

f fractures

stabilizes a fracture and allows you to move it immediately. A good example of this is in a femur fracture. A long nail inserted down the centre of the bone will allow you to get up and walk on the bone within a couple of weeks and this is much quicker than if it was allowed to heal by itself on traction and take 12 weeks. The healing, of course, goes on eventually even with the bone screwed and plated although it may take a little longer in some cases.

The disadvantage with this operative approach is that it involves anaesthetic and operation. There is a risk of introducing a germ and getting infection in the fracture which delays its healing and causes significant long-term problems.

• External fixator
This approach is relatively modern in its current form and is particularly valuable where there has been major injury not only to the bones but also the muscles and skin overlying them.

A common example of a fracture requiring external fixation is a fracture of the shin with a lot of injury to the skin around it. This regularly occurs in motorcycle accidents. In this technique, large pins are inserted into the shin bone above and below the fracture. These pins stick out through the skin and are held onto a bar on the outside of the body thus rigidly immobilizing the broken bone.

The advantages of the technique are all of those described in the section above but without the risk of an infection as the fracture itself is not actually operated on. The disadvantages are that the patient has to wear this 'scaffolding' around his or her leg. Also it won't be able to be kept on for long periods as the pins eventually loosen in the bone. However, by the time they do loosen the other wounds may have healed soundly enough for another form of treatment to be appropriate like a plaster cast.

• Percutaneous pinning
This is really a combination of internal and external fixation. Long pins are introduced through the skin just to temporarily fix a fracture. It is suitable where good hold and position of a fracture is needed but when you know the fracture will heal very quickly. Good examples are fractures in children and fractures in adults' fingers.

The pin can only stay in for four to six weeks but it often buys the surgeon enough time for the fracture to heal in a good position. The pins can then be removed as an outpatient procedure and another form of immobilization such as plaster applied until the fracture is soundly joined.

• There are one or two fractures which we still have no answer for and are unable to reconstruct. An example of this might be a very badly broken kneecap. However carefully it is put together the result is never as good as if it is removed completely. Some fractures of the neck of femur in the elderly person will fall into this category. Fracture at the very tip of the femur in the hip joint is highly unlikely to join up and therefore attempts to make it do so are never entertained. The broken end of the bone is removed and replaced with a metal one.

• Summary
It will be clear that bones, joints and tendons respond to use rather than disuse and a healing bone particularly needs stress to go through it in order for it to heal properly. Bone healing does take time and it is a very frustrating wait for many individuals. Nevertheless, although you may feel there is little you can do, those patients who throw themselves vigorously into a rehabilitation programme and remain as active as possible during their recovery do a lot better and get back to full activity much quicker than those who let the whole thing get on top of them and retire into their shell.

Dislocations

This is the serious problem of injury to your body where a joint is knocked out of place almost inevitably as a result of fairly high speed injury. It is common in sport. Finger dislocations frequently occur, and probably the biggest joint to regularly get dislocated is the shoulder. There may be associated fracturing. X-rays will be taken to check this and ensure that the joint has been put back properly.

Treatment

The treatment usually revolves around reducing the dislocation, i.e. putting the joint back, and this may well require an anaesthetic. You then need some form of immobilization afterwards to allow the ligaments, capsule and tendons around the joint to heal up as inevitably they are badly torn as the joint dislocates. This process usually takes at least three weeks to six weeks.

It is unwise to disregard the advice of your doctors about this and although you may think the joint feels a great deal better once it has been put back, if you don't allow the structures around the joint to heal thoroughly, they may become stretched and weak. The problem of recurrent dislocation is much more serious and can occur as a result of inappropriate early mobilization. Once the tissues have healed, however, gentle activity is built up often with the help of a physiotherapist. In most cases of dislocation a full functional recovery will occur in due course.

Other common injuries

We have dealt with the body's response to injury in the major tissue groups and some of the ways that they can be treated and rehabilitated. The commonest injuries have been used to illustrate these but the following common injuries also require special mention.

Whiplash (injury of the neck)

This is an extremely common injury and is almost solely the result of rear shunting motorcar accidents.

The neck is often a source of problems in many people but even in the perfectly normal neck a whiplash injury is very serious. Your head is very heavy and despite the strength of your neck muscles, they were never designed to withstand the force of sudden acceleration which occurs when a car strikes yours from behind. Your body is thrown forward and your neck left behind above the top of the seat. Typically people describe suddenly looking upwards at the car roof as their head whips backwards and then forwards again.

Often there are no immediate problems but within a few minutes or hours severe pain and stiffness occurs in the neck. X-rays are often needed to exclude a bony injury or major disruption or dislocation but these occur very rarely.

Nevertheless, the symptoms persist and may do so for many months and years. These injuries are notoriously slow to recover. Presumably most of the injury occurs at the ligaments and muscles of the neck but it is impossible to accurately pinpoint which muscles or ligaments are involved.

Treatment is usually anti-inflammatory tablets, a collar and physiotherapy but time is the eventual healer. Injuries of this nature do usually settle down eventually but in the meantime regular support in the form of a collar and then gradual build up of exercise is recommended. There is no evidence that cervical whiplash will lead to joint disease but osteoarthritis is common in the neck anyway.

One of the problems with whiplash injury is that as it is never your fault, there is a strong sense of indignation associated with it and this actually has a negative effect on your recovery.

Prevention

An important preventative measure is the use of properly fitted and adjusted head restraints. These are specifically designed to prevent whiplash injury and they certainly do help although they don't necessarily always prevent it. It is important to stress that they do need to be at the right height and fixed firmly. You should check with the car manufacturer's instructions about this. Rear collision injury, even at what appear to be quite slow speeds, can cause a nasty whiplash. It's very common and will inevitably happen to you or someone you know so take note of this advice.

Acute knee injury

This is one of the commonest causes of injury in the active person, especially contact sportsmen and women. Every Sunday afternoon the casualty departments of the country's hospitals are lined with muddy footballers with sore knees. Broadly speaking knee injuries occurring in skiing, football or squash are generally two-fold: either an acute injury to a ligament; or a tear of one of the menisci (knee cartilages).

Knee ligament injury

A violent strain put on the knee can damage any of the ligaments around it, in particular the inner or medial collateral ligament.

A simple sprain causes local pain, swelling or tenderness and will respond to rest, ice, ultrasound and time. A good functional result nearly always ensues.

If the violence is more severe, injury to other structures can occur, in particular the anterior cruciate ligament. It has been said that a torn anterior cruciate is the beginning of the end of the sportsperson's knee and this, unfortunately, is true in many cases. The ligament spans the joint preventing the shin bone (tibia) slipping forwards on the thigh bone (femur). When it is injured in sport there is immediate bleeding within the joint which swells up instantly or within a few moments. This is called a hemarthrosis and is tense and painful.

Unfortunately the anterior cruciate is exceptional in as much as it has no abilities to heal properly and even if the ends are sewn together surgically, the ligament never returns to its former strength. However, in some people this appears not to matter a great deal and if the blood is aspirated (drawn off through a needle) from the joint and they are treated with physiotherapy, they can get back to sport within a few weeks and appear to come to no long-term harm. Unfortunately, just as many appear to go on to get problems of instability and giving out of the knee. The difficulty that presents the surgeon is that it is impossible to tell who will do well and who badly.

Rupture of the anterior cruciate ligament is one of the commonest knee problems and the general feeling among surgeons now is that they should be treated by physiotherapy initially or a period of plaster and then physiotherapy. If late instability develops, reconstruction of the ligament by some means can be undertaken. Some surgeons favour early reconstruction but this is a fairly significant undertaking and it may be quite unnecessary in some of the cases. As you will appreciate it is an area of great controversy and there is no definite right or wrong answer.

Injury to a meniscus

A torn cartilage is also extremely common. It often occurs with an anterior cruciate tear and indeed it is more common if you have already torn your anterior cruciate ligament. The tear in the cartilage is not repairable at its free edge and in this sense the meniscus is somewhat like a tooth. It is clearly alive but if you damage it, it has no ability to regrow or heal up unless it's damaged right at its base. A cartilage tear may occur therefore as a sudden event and go on giving problems in the knee by jamming and locking, This will require surgical treatment to remove the torn fragment.

Arthroscopy

Nowadays diagnosis of anterior cruciate tears, and in particular torn cartilages, can be made with a telescope inserted into the joint under anaesthetic (an arthroscope). Torn cartilages can be diagnosed and removed through small puncture holes in the knee. This dramatically speeds up the process of rehabilitation after surgery and removal of a meniscus or part of one can be undertaken as a day case.

Nowadays attempts are being made to repair cartilages if they are torn at their base as it is known that the loss of a cartilage damages the knee and ultimately can lead to osteoarthritis of the knee.

Rehabilitation

Whether recovering from a torn ligament or cartilage, the importance of maintaining good muscle strength in the quadriceps and the hamstring muscles of the thigh cannot be over-emphasized. Similarly, if these muscles are in bad condition, you are more likely to injure the joint.

It is essential to have a regular programme of resistive exercises for quadriceps and hamstrings if you are going to take part in contact sports involving twisting and turning. This is also advisable for an annual skiing holiday where huge demands are made on the knee which may well not be fully prepared. Torn anterior cruciate ligament is very common on the ski slopes and can significantly impair future function and enjoyment of the sport. Although it is not always avoidable, good pre-holiday training may well reduce the risk of injury.

Rheumatoid and allied arthritis

Rheumatoid arthritis is a specific disease which affects the joints as well as many other organs in the body. It is very different from osteoarthritis in many respects. The cause of it is unknown but it is one of the so-called autoimmune diseases, i.e. there is an abnormality of the body's defence mechanisms which make it think that the joint lining is a foreign material. The body's defences attack it and this gives rise to grossly inflamed synovium (joint lining). This inflammation causes pain and swelling within the joint and ultimately damages it so badly that the shiny surface wears out and the joint may develop secondary wear and tear (osteo-) arthritis. Rheumatoid arthritis occurs in younger people than does osteoarthritis, often presenting in the mid- thirties with just one swollen joint which comes out of the blue. The disease usually spreads to affect other joints - no particular joints are immune from this condition. There are many drug treatments available which slow up the disease and occasionally cause remission over a period of time, but ultimately many patients with this distressing condition have to have surgery to either fuse or replace their diseased joints.

Physiotherapy to maintain movement and muscle strength is very important and is an area in which the patient can actively participate to get the best out of the uninvolved areas.

There are many rarer but allied inflammatory arthritides rather similar in presentation and course to rheumatoid. Psoriasis, which is not an uncommon skin disorder, can give rise to an inflammatory arthritis. Arthritis can also follow as an abnormal reaction to various infections particularly some sexually transmitted diseases.

Ankylosing spondylitis is another specific arthritis which tends to affect the spine and major joints. A feature of this disorder is remarkable stiffness. Joint replacement is often necessary in the late stages to give a range of pain-free movement in the hips, for example. In the early stages, however, physiotherapy and mobility exercises are essential.

Many of these specific diseases have associated self help organizations which are well worth seeking out and joining. They give valuable education about the disease and keep you abreast of current advances but also are a great source of support and advice.

Localized bone death

Bone is a living structure. It gets a blood supply like any other organ in the body. What sets it apart from other organs is its very slow rate of turnover and repair.

There are various well described situations and conditions in which for some reason the blood supply is damaged to a piece of bone and it dies back. This causes pain initially and although there may be little to see on early X-rays, the bone dies back and collapses down. A repair process eventually takes place but the eventual result is never as good as the initial bone shape.

Bone death (avascular necrosis, osteonecrosis) can occur as a result of a local injury, for example, in a fracture of the scaphoid, femoral neck or in the back of the foot, and this will clearly complicate fracture healing and lead to a worse result in the long term.

The condition may also occur as a result of decompression sickness and is therefore common in divers and mining workers, typically affecting the hips and shoulders. It can occur as a consequence of chronic alcoholism and a complication of treatment with steroids.

Osteonecrosis can also occur without any obvious predisposing cause and there are a group of conditions which occur in childhood. Presumably there is some abnormality in the growing bone which prevents proper vascular supply to an area. Possibly injury is also partly responsible. The child starts getting pain in the affected area. In some particular bones this is less important than others but a few of the commoner presentations of this condition are given in the left hand column .

Unfortunately there is no way of revascularizing (restoring the blood supply to) a dead segment of bone. The treatment for all of these is supportive, i.e. pain relief and rest initially and then a gradual build up of activity. In many of the smaller cases there is no long-term deficit, the child grows out of the problem and lives a normal active life in adulthood. Nevertheless, they can be a painful and unpleasant process to grow through at a time when the child is wanting to be very active.

• ***Perthes' disease***
In this condition the top of the femur in the hip joint dies back. It's the most serious of these childhood diseases as the subsequent hip may well be of the wrong shape when maturity is finished and osteoarthritis and pain can occur as a consequence. The treatment usually revolves around resting the area in the acute phase and then trying to keep the hip in a reasonable shape. Occasionally surgery is required for this. The results are variable depending on the severity of the disease but in some children a perfectly good result can be obtained.

• ***Schuerman's disease***
In this condition the vertebral bodies of the back are involved particularly the thoracic spine. This gives rise to local backache, a typical X-ray appearance and a rather round-shouldered appearance. By maturity no further extension of the disease occurs but this curvature of the spine persists.

• *There are a number of other bones typically affected and all with curious names: Freiberg's disease, involvement of a foot bone; Köhler's disease, involvement of a hind foot bone; Keinböck's disease, involvement of a bone in the wrist etc.*

Infection

Infection with viruses and bacteria can occur within bone, muscle and tendon. Fortunately these are now very unusual and are much less common than infections in, for example, the respiratory tract.

Infection of bone

Osteomyelitis used to be a much more common and serious problem, but with the advent of modern antibiotics this disease is now curable and, if properly treated, does not lead on to chronic bone infection as it used to do. The scourge of tuberculosis which caused debilitating bone infections as well as lung infections, has also been almost completely eradicated in this country. Only 50 years ago all the orthopaedic hospitals were full of patients with skeletal tuberculosis, and although this now does occasionally present, it's not the same devastating condition as it used to be. Sadly, it is still common in the underdeveloped countries of the world.

Probably the commonest cause of infection in the bones nowadays stems from infected fracture after serious injury either as a complication of internal fixation of fractures or as a result of the fracture having serious injury to the soft parts over it.

Chronic infected fractures are still a major problem for a small number of people and require prolonged antiobiotic treatment as well as often repeated surgical operations. Nevertheless, with modern techniques these can often be cured although it may take several years.

Tumours

Primary cancer of the bone and related structures of the musculo-skeletal system is thankfully very rare. The bone, however, is a very common site for secondary spread of cancers from other areas, notably the lung, breast, thyroid, prostate and kidney.

In these much commoner conditions the tumour spreads from the original site and settles and grows in the bone. This may occur without any signs or symptoms whatsoever but may cause local pain and X-rays usually define the problem. Sometimes the first sign of trouble is a fracture occurring through the tumorous area. This is known as a pathological fracture and can occur with relatively minor injury or apparently spontaneously.

These pathological fractures do not heal up as well as 'normal' fractures and often need treating by internal fixation to stabilize them. The area can then be treated, if appropriate, by radiotherapy.

Alternative approaches

Your environment, work, lifestyle, personal relationships, nutrition and mental state all play their part in determining the general level of health of your active body. This is recognized by practitioners of both orthodox and alternative medicine. By alerting you to the way these factors affect your health, alternative therapies can help you stay well. If problems arise they see them within the context of you-as-a-whole, rather than simply as a set of symptoms, and they work with you to mobilize your body's own defences to combat them. Because they're concerned with the causes which underlie problems, alternative therapies tend to take longer to show results - but their effects may be more permanent, too.

The value of alternative therapies - particularly their emphasis on maintaining good health - is increasingly being recognized by orthodox practitioners and much of the material you have already read on your active body advises self-help. Some of the 'alternative' practices that were regarded as cranky or extreme only a few years ago are widely accepted and used now.

Acupuncture

Traditional Chinese medicine says that a vital energy called chi flows through our bodies via meridians (vertical pathways). Each meridian is linked to a specific organ or function. The meridians are related to each other by cross-channels so that all organs and tissues have access to chi. If the flow of chi through the body is disrupted, diseases and ailments result. Chi is activated by the body's life-forces, Yin and Yang, which must be in perfect balance if they are to maintain the flow of chi. Health, then, depends on a free flow of chi and balance between the forces of Yin and Yang.

A number of physical and emotional factors can restrict the flow of chi and thus affect internal organs or their functions, and the acupuncturist's holistic approach to diagnosis will seek to identify them. Some may be remedied by changes in eating, sleeping or exercise patterns; others by helping the patient deal more effectively with stress, pressure or negative emotions.

By stimulating specific points on the body's meridians by means of small, sterile needles, the acupuncturist can help to restore the proper flow of chi throughout the body. The process is usually painless, though you may experience a tingling sensation along the meridian being treated. Symptoms usually disappear gradually over a course of treatment, but may get worse before they improve.

One area where acupuncture has been found to be especially useful is in the relief of pain and it can be of great value to people suffering from arthritis and chronic back pain. It is thought that stimulation of acupuncture points results in the release of endorphins, which are the body's own pain-relieving substances. It may also be that stimulating large nerve-fibres blocks the pain impulses carried by smaller ones.

Acupressure
This is basically acupuncture without needles and, unlike acupuncture, you can do it to yourself. It involves putting pressure on certain points either with your fingers, or the blunt end of a ballpoint pen.

The Alexander technique

The muscles and bones of your body are designed to interact so that you can move easily and without strain. Unfortunately, you can get into habits of behaviour and movement that throw this balance out of true, and although these habits come to seem normal and natural, they can actually cause all sorts of problems. The Alexander Technique aims to help you relearn how to use your body properly.

On a one-to-one basis, an Alexander teacher works with you by gently realigning and manipulating your body, gradually making you aware of how it feels when it's used properly. You're shown correct, balanced ways of sitting, standing and lying down. Movements are accompanied by a set of directions, which become familiar over time. Learning is transferred to 'real' life when you can automatically monitor your own posture and movements, correcting them when they're faulty. This may take up to 30 sessions.

The Alexander Technique is particularly effective for dealing with tension headaches, low back pain and stress.

Diet and arthritis

Avoiding obesity, and the strain this puts on your muscles and bones, makes sense whether you suffer from an arthritic condition or not. Keep control of your weight, if you have any symptoms of arthritis. You might like to try:

- *Avoiding meat: vegetarians seem to suffer less from osteoarthritis. This seems to have something to do with maintaining the body's proper calcium balance.*
- *Avoiding refined carbohydrates: they've been robbed of essential nutrients during processing, and may affect the overall balance of vitamins and minerals in your body.*
- *Avoiding fats: some studies suggest they may play a part in rheumatoid arthritis.*
- *Finding out whether your symptoms are worse after eating certain foods: you may be allergic to them without knowing it. Some common foods implicated in American studies include citrus fruits, eggs, milk, cheese, grain products. If you do restrict your intake, remember that you may need vitamin or mineral supplements to compensate.*
- *Extra vitamin C, vitamin E to relieve any pain, and increased zinc (especially for rheumatoid arthritis). Consult your medical adviser.*

Herbalism

Herbal treatments have been used all over the world for thousands of years, and some of the most powerful drugs used in orthodox medicine today are based on plants and plant extracts. Some plants are poisonous or have unwelcome side-effects, but medical herbalists have access to extensive research which enables them to identify exactly the right treatment for the individual patient.

Like other alternative practitioners, the medical herbalist bases treatment on a holistic approach, aimed at assisting natural healing and restoring you to balanced health. Because herbalism treats you rather than your ailments, a herbalist needs to build up a complete picture of your health and lifestyle and search for clues to the causes of any problems. What's appropriate for you may be the wrong thing for somebody else, even if you seem to be experiencing similar things. Prescriptions vary, and depend on what's needed to restore good health; they may be altered over time according to how you react to them. Self-help measures may also be suggested, and adjustments recommended to your diet, exercise, work and social life.

Herbal remedies use extracts from whole plants, not just their active ingredients. This reduces the incidence of unwanted side-effects that may arise when the active constituents are used in isolation. The result is that herbal medicine tends to be gentler, safer and less disturbing to the body than orthodox remedies - but it may be a while before you notice its effects.

Dosage of some herbal remedies is strictly controlled by law, because many plants may be toxic. Other medicines can have powerful effects. Medical herbalists often work together with practitioners in other alternative disciplines, and with orthodox doctors.

Homoeopathy

Homoeopathy works on the principle that 'like cures like'. You are treated with tiny doses of medication that would cause your symptoms in a healthy person, and which stimulate your body's own healing mechanisms. Many homoeopaths are also trained in orthodox medicine and, like orthodox medics, they recognize and treat patterns of symptoms - but in a different way.

Homoeopaths regard the body as a complete, living whole. When it's disturbed in any way, coordinated action is necessary to protect or restore homoeostasis (balance). This action is controlled by what homoeopaths call the 'vital force', which produces symptoms as it strives for homoeostasis. A disease, therefore, is a collection of symptoms that occur when the sick body is trying to heal itself. Homoeopathy seeks to enhance those symptoms - the body's natural reaction to some kind of stress - and help them work more effectively to promote healing.

During homoeopathic treatment, the practitioner carefully monitors how your body responds before determining further treatment. If you consult a homoeopath, you may be advised to discontinue other forms of therapy as they can confuse the picture. It's not uncommon, however, to combine homoeopathic treatment with some form of manipulative therapy.

In your first interview with a homoeopath, the idea will be to build up a picture of your symptoms or disease. This will then be matched against the picture of the available remedies. The remedy whose total picture most closely matches the picture of your symptoms is the one which will be prescribed.

Although some homoeopathic medicines are available over the counter they should not be taken unless they are specifically prescribed by a homoeopath. A practitioner can also advise you about self-help based on homoeopathic theory. Coffee, peppermint, eucalyptus, camphor and menthol all affect the action of homoeopathic remedies, so should be avoided while you're having homoeopathic treatment.

Hypnotherapy

By allowing contact with your unconscious - which is constantly monitoring all the physical and psychological functions of both mind and body - hypnotherapy can be

• ***Herbalism***

Herbal treatment is also based on individual symptoms, so a medical herbalist is the best person to advise. Parsley tea, which is a diuretic that helps the body flush out poisons, can be made by adding 5 ml (1 teaspoon) of chopped parsley to a cupful of boiling water. Cover and leave to cool; strain and drink at intervals during the day (but avoid this if you're pregnant). A herbalist may also suggest extract of willow and primula combined with yeast extract as an anti-inflammation preparation without harmful side-effects. Herbs may also be used in ointments and liniments.

• Laying on of hands
In cases where back pain is the result of muscular tension caused by either physical or mental stress rather than a skeletal problem, remedial or therapeutic massage can be extremely helpful. Healers (those who practise 'faith healing' or 'laying on of hands') are often successful in relieving pain.

used to modify the ways you react to particular stimuli and how you behave in particular situations. It is basically a process designed to achieve deep concentration combined with a diminished awareness of your surroundings. It is not something that can be done 'to' you against your will. It is particularly helpful in alleviating conditions which are caused by stress.

Over four or five sessions, the hypnotherapist works with you to explore and alter specific ingrained patterns of thought and behaviour. For example, if you habitually react to any kind of stress by becoming tense and anxious - or by lighting a cigarette - the hypnotherapist can help you recognize and deal with such situations more constructively.

The hypnotic 'trance' is akin to deep relaxation, and you become more receptive to suggestions than you would normally be. It's as if your critical faculty - which makes your conscious mind reject uncomfortable ideas - has been switched off. Depending on why you've sought help, the practitioner will suggest new ways of behaving or reacting to situations you normally find difficult. It may take a while to alter deep-rooted patterns of thought or behaviour, especially if the reasons for them are complex, but this process will usually be rather quicker with the help of hypnotherapy than during one of the 'talking' therapies where your conscious mind may edit what you say.

One useful side-effect of hypnotherapy may well be that you learn relaxation techniques that you can easily apply when you feel yourself becoming stressed in any way. It can also help alter the way you experience and respond to pain.

Manipulative therapies

Osteopathy and chiropractic are based on the similar theory that abnormalities of your skeletal system can adversely affect the health of the whole of the rest of your body - including the lungs, heart, stomach, intestines, bladder and uterus. Where they differ is that osteopaths treat structural imbalances by levering and twisting the body, while chiropractors treat the bones separately by specific thrusts. Both base their work on orthodox concepts of anatomy and physiology, may well use X-rays to help them arrive at a diagnosis (though chiropractors are more likely to do this), and take a holistic approach to health care. They accept that problems can also be caused by genetic factors as well as dietary, environmental, psychological and bacterial ones: though treatment can relieve symptoms in these cases, it won't cure.

Most people initially consult an osteopath or chiropractor because they're experiencing back problems, or discomfort in other joints and muscles. Treatment is often very effective. Orthodox medicine is increasingly recognizing the value of manipulative therapy in relieving both chronic (long-lasting) and acute back pain, and many mainstream doctors are quite happy to refer their patients to qualified osteopaths and chiropractors for treatment.

Before embarking on treatment, the practitioner asks you about your medical history and gives you a complete physical examination that includes watching how you stand and move. Both osteopaths and chiropractors can be extremely skilful at identifying and treating tiny misalignments in the spine or in other parts of the body which result in pain that may be felt far from the site of what's causing it. As with other alternative therapies, the idea is to isolate and treat the cause of your problem rather than simply the problem itself.

Osteopathic treatment may also include deep muscular massage, postural re-education and relaxation.

Because manipulative therapies can be dangerous if not properly carried out, it's important to ensure that your practitioner is properly qualified and experienced.

Massage

Regular massage of your body's soft tissues - your muscles and ligaments - stimulates the circulation of the blood and the functioning of the nervous system. It can soothe headaches, relieve any tension and stress in the body, relax taut muscles and help create a feeling of calm and well-being. Swedish massage is based on rhythmic, continual movement, while the Japanese Shiatsu system combines massage with acupressure to the body's meridians (see Acupuncture, page 88). Simple massage techniques are not difficult to learn: you can massage some parts of your body yourself, a partner can do it for you, or you can turn to a qualified practitioner.

Aromatherapy

Aromatic oils are sometimes used for massage. This technique is based on the fact that smells can influence your emotional state, and that individual oils can have a therapeutic effect on your body. Essential oils, which are the 'neat' form of any scent, can be both strong and expensive so a couple of drops may be added to a 'carrier' oil - a teaspoon of vegetable oil, for example.

Naturopathy

Fresh air and sunlight, exercise, rest and relaxation, good nutrition, hygiene and hydrotherapy (water therapy) lie at the heart of naturopathy's commonsense approach to health care. It's basically a way of practising preventive medicine - making sure that you stay healthy enough to enable your body to fight off any problems that might arise.

Like other 'alternative' practitioners, naturopaths believe that both good health - and problems - are dependent on a combination of factors. Symptoms of illness, they say, can be indications of your body's efforts to reject disease and get rid of the effects of a lifestyle that's unhealthy in some way. They also believe in the body's power to heal itself, provided that it's properly maintained and treated.

Many of naturopathy's basic theories have now become so familiar, and so widely accepted, that many of the self-help suggestions you'll find throughout this book - and recommended by orthodox practitioners - are based on them.

Naturopaths adopt a holistic approach to diagnosis and treatment, believing that individuals function on structural, biochemical and emotional levels. If there's a problem in one area, it can have far-reaching effects on the others. An initial consultation with a naturopath involves a detailed medical history and a physical examination, with the aim of building up a total picture of the way your physical and emotional lifestyle is affecting your health. Any treatment includes guidelines on how you can maintain good health, and these are usually so straightforward that you can incorporate them simply into your way of life. Naturopaths often work closely with practitioners of manipulative therapies, and their treatment for some conditions may begin with a short fast to cleanse the body of toxins (poisons).

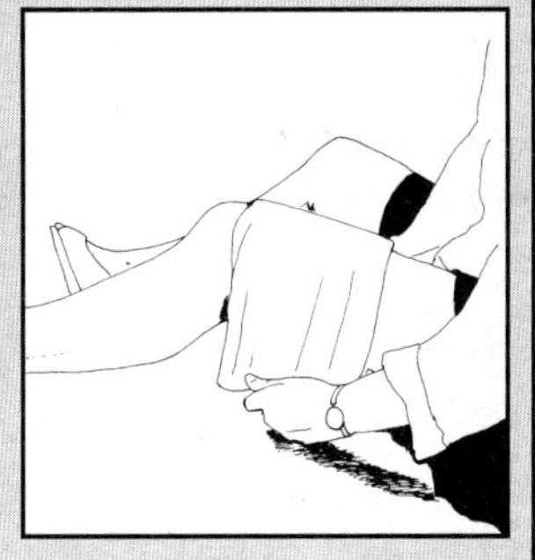

Naturopaths, who practise a commonsense approach to staying well, recommend hydrotherapy (water therapy) for general aches, pains and stiffness: soak a towel in hot water until it feels hot, wring it out, then apply it to the site of the pain for three minutes. Follow it by a cold one applied for one minute. Repeat this hot-and-cold fomentation routine for 20-30 minutes, at least once a day, and keep active to relieve any stiffness.

The naturopathic approach to the prevention and management of arthritis, which is based on a period of fasting followed by a strictly-controlled vegetarian diet, is said to have been extremely effective in cases of both rheumatoid arthritis and osteoarthritis. Homoeopaths can prescribe a number of remedies, which vary from person to person depending on individual symptoms.

Other titles in the series

Your Pregnancy and Childbirth (ISBN 0 245-55068-2)
Your Sex Life (ISBN 0 245-55067-4)
Your Heart and Lungs (ISBN 0 245-55069-0)

Available, Spring 1990
Your Mind (ISBN 0 245-60008-6)
Your Diet (ISBN 0 245-60009-4)
Your Skin (ISBN 0 245-60010-8)
Your Child (ISBN 0 245-60011-6)

Available, Autumn 1990
Your Female Body (ISBN 0 245-60012-4)
Your Senses (ISBN 0 245-60013-2)
A-Z of Conditions and Drugs (ISBN 0 245-60014-0)

Useful organizations

Arthritis and Rheumatism Council for Research
41 Eagle Street
London WC1R 4AR

British Chiropractic Association
Premier House
10 Greycoat Place
London SW1P 1SB

Council for Acupuncture (umbrella group for the main colleges)
Suite One
191A Cavendish Square
London W1M 9AD

General Council and Register of Osteopaths
56 London Street
Reading
Berkshire RG21 4SQ

National Institute of Medical Herbalists
41 Hatherley Road
Winchester
Hampshire SO22 6RR

PRIME HEALTH
Private Medical Insurers
Prime House
Barnett Wood Lane
Leatherhead
Surrey KT22 7BS
0372 386060